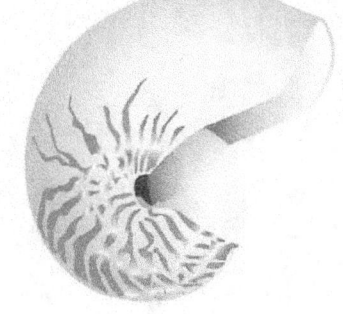 **C**oastal
Marine
Institute

University of Alaska

Proceedings of a Workshop on Hydrological Modeling of Freshwater Discharge from Alaska's Arctic Coast

Jia Wang
Principal Investigator

Final Report
OCS Study MMS 2006-043

July 2006

Minerals Management Service
Department of the Interior

and the

School of Fisheries & Ocean Sciences

University of Alaska Fairbanks

Table of Contents

List of Figures

Appendices

Hydrological Modeling of the Mackenzie Basin using WATFLOOD and WATCLASS in MAGS:

A Hydrological Digital Elevation Model for Freshwater Discharge into the Gulf of Alaska:

List of Tables

List of Acronyms

ETOPO5 – Eeath TOPOgraphy – (5 minute) digital average land and sea floor.

GTOPO30 – Global TOPOgraphy – (30 second) derived from digital elevation model (DEM) average land and sea floor.

NCEP/NCAR – National Center for Environmental Prediction/National Center for Atmospheric Research

ECMWF/ERA40 – European Center for Medium-range Weather Forecasts/ECMWF Re-Analysis of 40 years.

Abstract

A workshop on Hydrological Modeling of Freshwater Discharge from Alaska's Arctic Coast was held at the International Arctic Research Center (IARC), University of Alaska Fairbanks (UAF) on 7–8 October 2004 (http://www.iarc.uaf.edu/workshops/hydro_mod_workshop_04/). This workshop was sponsored by the Minerals Management Service (MMS)/U.S. Department of the Interior and Coastal Marine Institute/UAF, hosted by the IARC. One of the objectives of this workshop was to bring modelers and observationalists together to discuss strategies for state-of-the-art hydrological modeling north of the Brooks Range. The workshop highlighted approaches to medium-range, regional hydrological modeling that could be applied to the North Slope region, which drains into the nearshore Beaufort and Chukchi seas, affecting seasonal landfast ice, coastal circulation, and water mass properties. A second objective was to promote discussion of the following topics:

- *Climate variability and its impacts on hydrological cycle in the Arctic*
- *Collection and archival of hydrological datasets in Alaska*
- *Hydrological modeling approaches on the North Slope*
- *Hydrology-related sea ice, oceanography, and geochemistry*

The workshop had three research themes: 1) Climate and variability and its impacts, 2) Hydrological observations and modeling, and 3) Sea ice, oceanography, and geochemistry. There were 28 participants (23 presentations). Each theme had a rapporteur to chair the discussions and summarize the recommendations at the end of the workshop. The workshop produced recommendations, which are valuable for MMS needs and may be used as a guideline to arctic hydrological modeling and related research areas.

The workshop focused on precedents in data processing, hydrological modeling, and field observations: including needs, scientific and economic issues, and possible solutions in this region. The participants included scientists and managers from academic institutions, governmental laboratories, the state, borough, and local communities.

Introduction

This hydrological modeling workshop is directly related to the MMS framework issue "Modeling studies of environmental, social, economic, or cultural processes related to OCS gas and oil activities in order to improve scientific predictive capabilities." MMS is interested in freshwater runoff because it is important locally in the coastal Beaufort Sea: it enhances breakup of nearshore ice and affects release of spilled oil from landfast ice, water mass properties, and density-driven currents of the nearshore shelf, such as coastal current along Alaska's Arctic coast (Weingartner et al. 1998; Fig. 1). Furthermore, changes in timing and amounts of river runoff to the arctic shelves may affect the ocean circulation (Weingartner 1998; Wang et al. 1999).

There are six sites in the North Slope region currently being gaged (http://akrfc.arh.noaa.gov/view hydrology): the Kuparuk River, the Colville River at Umiat and at the river mouth, the Ikpikpuk River near Barrow, the Sagavanirktok River, and Fish Creek. Although a fairly comprehensive observation network has been put in place on the watersheds of these rivers, it covers a small portion of the entire Alaska Arctic coast. For example, the North Slope Hydrology Research Projects (the Kuparuk River Watershed Studies), conducted by the Water Environmental and Resources Center (WERC) of UAF, focuses on small-scale basin watershed (http://www.uaf.edu/water/projects/NorthSlope/northslope.html). There have also been some small-scale observational studies in the North Slope Region (http://www.uaf.edu/water/faculty.html).

A vast region remains ungaged (see Fig. 2). The percentage of the discharge that is ungaged has not been quantified; this portion drains into the Alaska's Arctic in a manner of line sources (Wang et al. 1999, 2004; Carmack 2000; Jin and Wang 2003). Thus, there is a great need to focus on the existing hydrological observation and known processes to quantify river runoff along the Arctic coast (Kane et al. 1996, 1997; McNamara et al. 1997, 1998; Hinzman et al. 2000). Known factors influencing runoff include climate variability (temperature and precipitation, etc.), terrain elevation, terrain ground cover (vegetation types), evaporation, soil type and

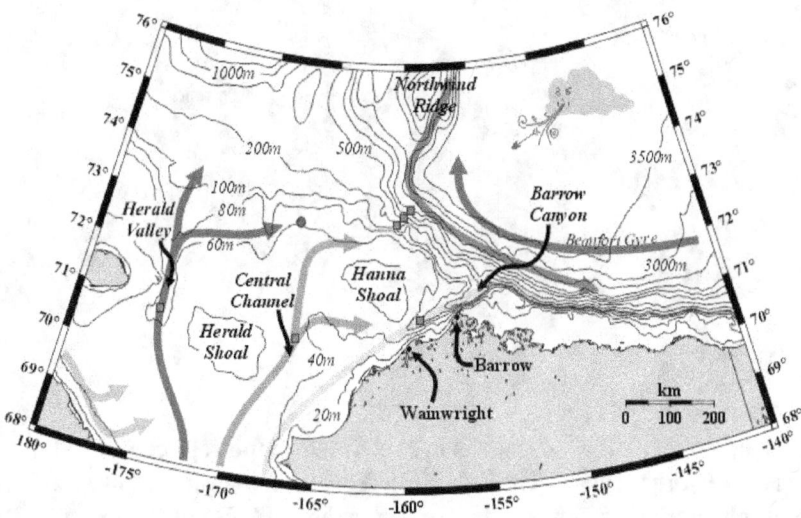

Figure 1. A schematic diagram for coastal circulation in the Chukchi-Beaufort Seas (light blue: Alaskan Coast Current with the origin of freshwater). (Courtesy of Tom Weingartner).

permafrost distribution, snow drifting and melting, and glacier melting. Unlike the steep terrain along the Gulf of Alaska (Wang et al. 2004), the North Slope of Alaska is more complex because there exists not only surface runoff, but also aquifer and ground water discharge due to its relatively flat terrain. Although there have been digital elevation data collected with 1 km or finer spatial resolution from the North Slope and six hydrological gages north of the Brooks Range, there has not yet been a high resolution digital elevation model (DEM)-based hydrological model constructed for the region to calculate freshwater discharge into the Arctic Ocean from Alaska's Arctic coast.

Obviously, a high-resolution, large-scale DEM-based hydrological model (Fig. 2) would fill the gap between the small-scale observation studies and coarse-resolution pan-Arctic modeling. There-fore, it was an especially appropriate time for this workshop to put forward new ideas to stimulate a fresh modeling effort in the region. This interdis-ciplinary research would involve Arctic climate change (Thompson and Wallace 1998; Wang and Ikeda 2000, 2001; Ikeda et al. 2001; Wu et al. 2006), atmospheric circulation, temperature and precipitation (Walsh et al. 1998; Yang et al. 2001, 2002), hydrology (Kane et al. 1996, 1997, 1998; McNamara et al. 1997, 1998), and coastal circula-tion (Weingartner et al. 1998; Wang et al. 1999).

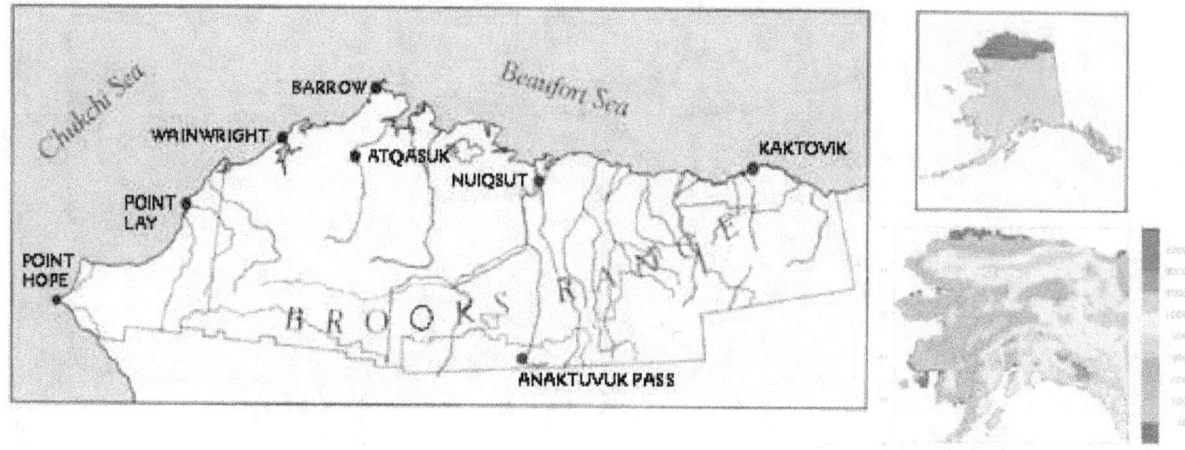

Figure 2. (Left and right upper) River networks in the North Slope region and outer continental shelf in the Beaufort and Chukchi seas. (Right lower) Terrain distribution based on the ETOPO5 (9.2-km) dataset, a much coarser resolution dataset than the GTOPO30 (1 km). The Brooks Range divides the North Slope watershed from the Yukon River watershed south of the Brooks Range. The Mackenzie River watershed in Canada is not shown.

Objectives

The objectives of this workshop were to:

- Review precedents in hydrological observations, data archives and analysis, and modeling of freshwater discharge (including river runoff from numerous creeks and streams due to snow and glacier melting).

- Review the impacts of climate variability on hydrology in the North Slope, and possible connections between hydrology, sea ice, and oceanography

- Lay out strategies for hydrological observation and modeling, particularly for implementing a high-resolution DEM-based hydrological model, which will incorporate the first-order hydrological processes (precipitation, energy balance, aquifer/land processes) to estimate freshwater discharge into the Arctic Ocean primarily along the Beaufort-Chukchi sea coasts.

- Make recommendations to MMS for future research, including atmospheric forcing, hydrology-related sea ice, oceanography, and biogeochemistry, which would also benefit water resource management by the State of Alaska, North Slope Borough, and local communities.

Workshop Strategies

Atmosphere, hydrology/oceanography, and sea ice are important components of the Arctic climate system. Atmospheric circulation, precipitation, and temperature fields are considered forcing functions of hydrological models in terms of heat budget and energy balance. Thus, atmospheric circulation variability or climate change will directly impact the hydrological cycle in regional, basin, and global scales. The commonly-used datasets are either the reanalysis (such as NCEP/NCAR and ECMWF/ERA40) or global model outputs. Figure 3 shows a global model simulation and projection of precipitation in the North Slope for the period of 1960–2100. It indicates the weather in North Slope became wetter in the last four decades (1960–2000), and will continue so in the next 100 years. It is also seen that there is decadal and multi-decadal variability in precipitation, which will result in decadal and multi-decadal variability in freshwater runoff, and eventually lead to Arctic climate change on the similar quasi-decadal time scales (Wang et al. 2005).

8

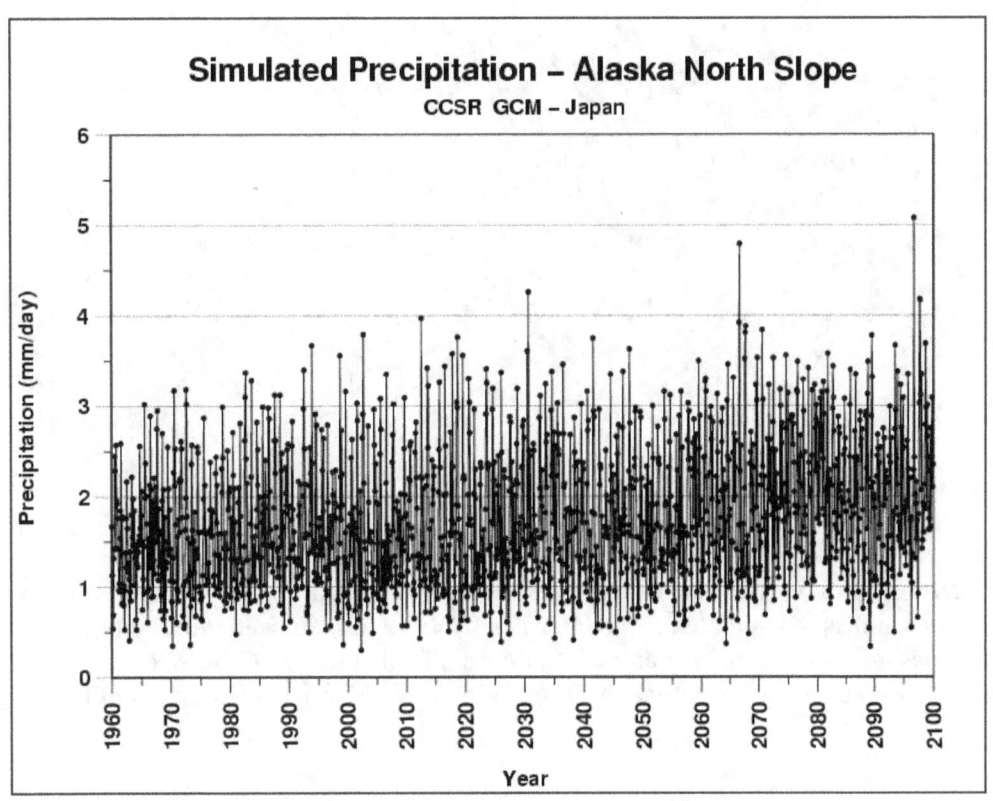

Figure 3. The time series of Alaska North Slope precipitation simulated by the CCSR/NIES/ FRCGC climate model of Japan (Courtesy of J. Walsh). (CCSR-Climate Change System Research-Tokyo University, NIES—National Institute of Environmental Studies, Japan, FRCGC—Frontier Research Center for Global Change, Japan).

Arctic warming may be an important trigger for wetter weather in the Arctic (Polyakov et al. 2003). The warmer climate also melts North Slope glaciers (such as McCall Glacier) and thaws the frozen ground or permafrost, leading to an increase in freshwater runoff along the Arctic Coast. Other important parameters include snow cover and its albedo. Thus, measuring albedo of snow cover using satellites is important for having a large spatial coverage.

Reanalysis data and global model outputs are used for hydrological modeling in a downscaling process. Thus, an observational network using meteorology stations in the North Slope region becomes an urgent task for validating the downscaling forcing fields based on reanalysis and large-scale model output.

Hydrological modeling of the North Slope watershed and in the pan Arctic region was con-

ducted (Bowling et al. 2000) in a coarse resolution (50 km). In the North Slope an example can be shown in Figure 4 in a very coarse resolution grid. Seasonal cycle of freshwater runoff can be reasonably simulated (right panel of Fig. 4). Nevertheless, detailed watershed information, river network, and small-scale processes were missing.

There are some small-scale basin simulations in a single small watershed on the North Slope (such as Kuparuk Basin), and also in a single large watershed elsewhere in the Arctic (such as Mackenzie Basin, Lena Basin, etc.) (Fig. 4). In the Gulf of Alaska watershed, a medium-scale DEM-based hydrological model was developed with a 4 km resolution (Wang et al. 2004), which (Fig. 5) successfully simulates the river runoff and line-source runoff (ungaged small streams, rivers, snow-melt discharge, etc.) from 1958–1998. The line-source runoff accounts for 76% of total runoff in the re-

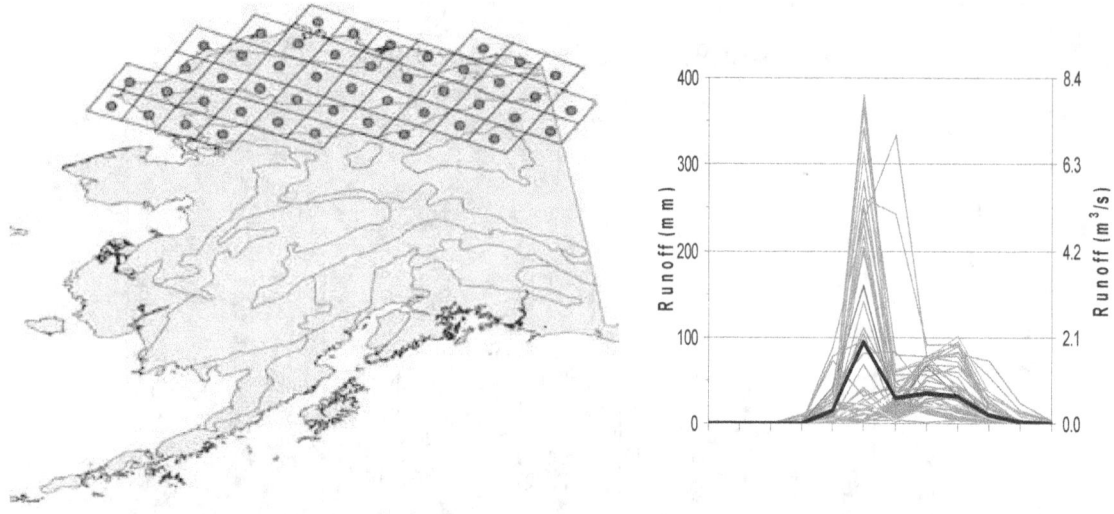

Figure 4. Left panel: A North Slope hydrological model grid. Right panel: Seasonal cycle (from January to December) of simulated freshwater runoff. In Lakes and wetlands, 60 to 74% of snow melt water goes into storage and is not immediately available for runoff. Between 50 and 64% of the stored meltwater is depleted by evaporation from open water areas (Courtesy of L. Bowling).

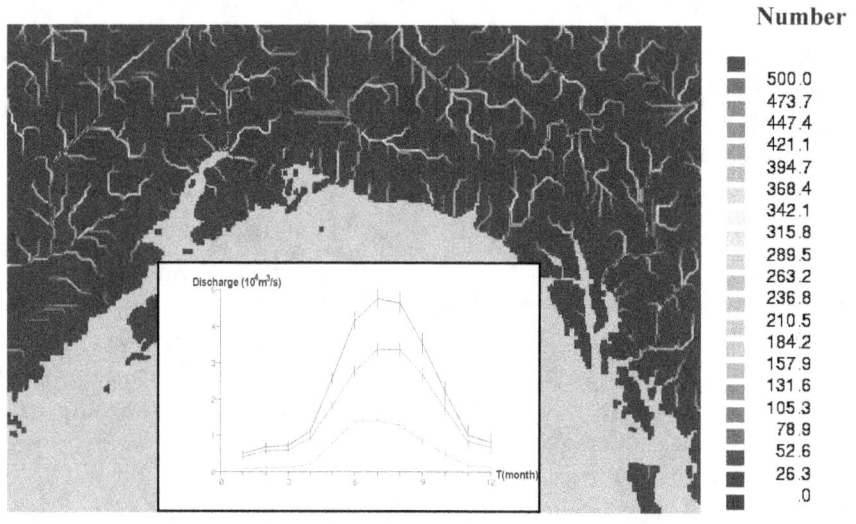

Figure 5. The Gulf of Alaska watershed number at every grid point before the streams become constant in the study area. The watershed number denotes units of total grid point area (km^2). The inserted figure shows the model simulated monthly climatology (seasonal cycle) of freshwater discharge derived from the 41-year simulations (1958–1998) and standard deviations (vertical bars). Black line is the total discharge into the Gulf of Alaska; the blue line is the line source, and the red is the point source (Wang et al. 2004).

gion, which is the major forcing mechanism forming and maintaining the Alaska Coastal Current.

Observational studies of single river basins or the remote sensing technique that has been applied to measure runoff in one river can be used to validate a model. Data from the extensive USGS stream gaging network across Alaska (Fig. 6) can be used for analysis and validation of any hydrological models. Considering the limited coverage in the North Slope, a medium-scale hydrological model is an ideal candidate to fill the gap between the large-scale modeling and small-scale single basin modeling, given that observation in the North Slope is scarce. The North Slope model will consider first-order hydrological processes, such as

terfaces is greatly altered by sea ice and freshwater conditions. In particular, landfast ice conditions are determined not only by the atmospheric conditions, but also by freshwater runoff and ocean circulation.

In addition, freshwater runoff can generate oceanic fronts in the Chukchi and Beaufort seas, and produce coastal ocean current due to the horizontal density gradient (Fig. 8). A coupled ice-ocean model can reproduce such coastal freshening and the coastal current (Maslowski et al. 2000; Wang et al. 2002).

River discharge from the North Slope is a driver that brings terrestrial organic carbon and trace metals into the ocean, which modifies the nearshore environment in terms of biogeochemistry. Sea ice

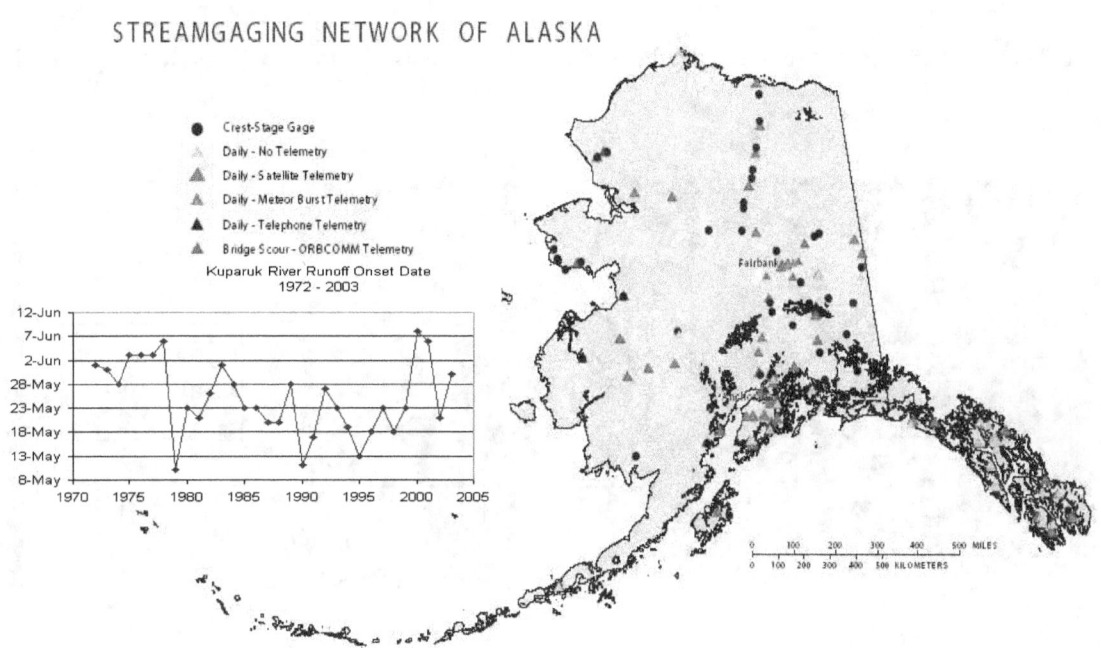

Figure 6. The U.S. Geological Survey streamgaging network of Alaska (Courtesy of D. Myers) Inserted is an example of the time series of Kuparuk River runoff onset date from 1972–2003.

lakes and wetlands, snow albedo, energy balance, and aquifer/land processes, etc.

Dispersal of river discharge into the Arctic seas can significantly influence the sea-ice environment, because the Arctic coastal zone is a multi-phase boundary: atmosphere-sea ice-ocean-land interfaces (Fig. 6; Eicken et al. submitted). Exchange of heat, moisture, and momentum between the in-

formation and advection will further redistribute the materials into the deep basins (Wang et al. 2003). Thus, sources of freshwater (Fig. 9) including river discharge, the Bering Sea inflow, and sea ice melting are key dynamic processes for the nearshore Beaufort-Chukchi seas ice-ocean dynamics (Kawai et al. 2005; MacDonald et al. 1999, 2005).

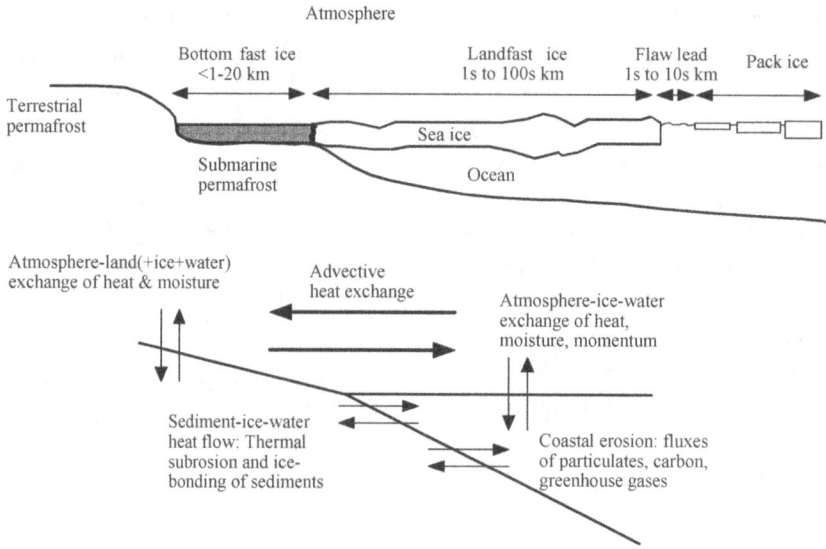

Figure 7. The Arctic coastal zone can be defined as a multi-phase boundary (Courtesy of H. Eicken).

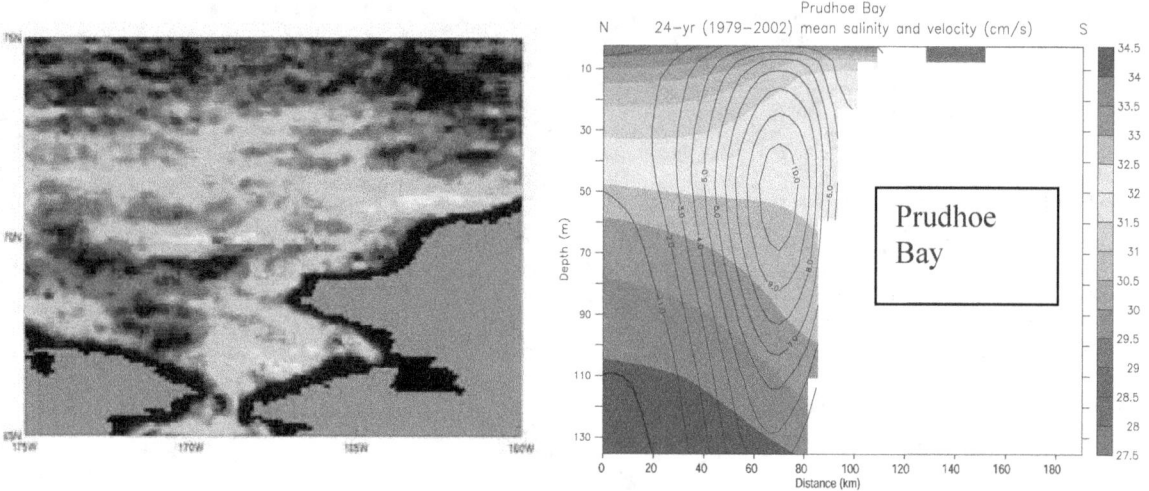

Figure 8. Left panel: Frequency of oceanic SST fronts in August as determined by remote sensing data (Courtesy of I. Belkin); Right panel: 9 km ice-ocean model-simulated coastal current and salinity in the section of Prudhoe Bay (Courtesy of Maslowski).

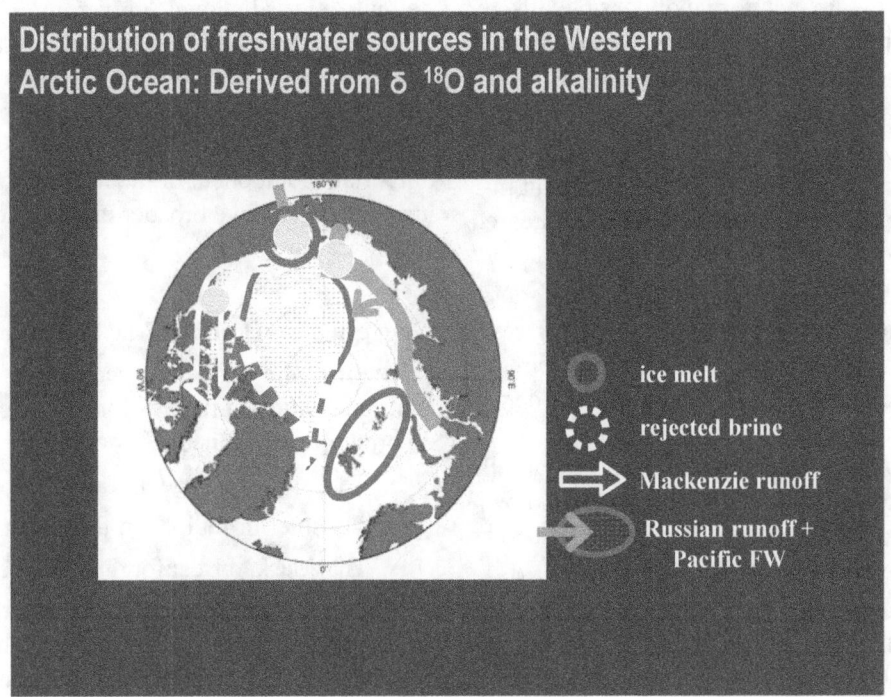

Figure 9. Western Arctic freshwater sources derived from $\delta 18^0$ and alkalinity (courtesy of M. Kawai).

Working Group Recommendations

Theme 1: Climate Variability and its Impacts (original records)

General

The discussion focused on the requirements of terrestrial hydrology for climate forcing parameters, in particular for the MMS context and in general for the broader Alaska context. Caryn Smith outlined general MMS requirements, which include nearshore management and near-coastal discharge and currents for the North Alaska regional setting. MMS is interested in work that provides insight into theoretical underpinnings as well as derivation of practical applications. Given the general workshop theme of terrestrial hydrological modeling on Alaska's North Slope and elsewhere, discussion turned to identifying climate forcing data best suited to hydrological modeling needs, as well as how best to adapt climate data for these purposes. This included observational data and climate model data, both predictive and reanalysis.

Specific Themes Within the Discussion

Observational data: Climate observational data are important in hydrological monitoring for several reasons:

    a. These data help to establish understanding of essential processes;

    b. Data are used to build process and system models;

    c. Data also serve to verify models.

The arctic regions in general suffer from a lack of climate observational data. For the context of the North Slope, three specific shortcomings were identified.

- The interior of the North Slope is virtually without climate observational support. Specific areas have been instrumented as part of projects, such as the Colville and McCall Rivers, but such efforts are limited spatially (by design they cover only a single catchment) as well as temporally. The interior of the North Slope requires the establishment of long-term monitoring, as well as identification

13

and follow-up monitoring of possible different, previously un-instrumented, regional eco-types within the North Slope.

- The Brooks mountain range, which provides the source waters for many drainage basins in the North Slope, is also virtually without instrumentation. This, too, should be addressed with the establishment of an instrumentation/ monitoring program.

- The coastal region, although possessing several weather stations, is less of a problem than the interior, which still lacks sufficient density to be fully descriptive. Furthermore, in some cases existing coastal stations, specifically the five automatic weather stations operated by MMS in the Deadhorse vicinity, are due to be shut down in fall 2006.

Scale discrepancies: Matching spatial and temporal scales between climate forcing data and the needs of the hydrological community is challenging because climate data is usually available only at broad spatial scales, whereas the interest of the hydrological community lies with processes operating at relatively fine spatial scales. This issue may be identified for climate data obtained from both observational sources and modeled sources.

- Observational data can be scale limited due to a lack of site representativeness. For example, data obtained from a coastal station, a typical situation for northern Alaska, is ill-suited to drive an interior watershed model because the data do not represent conditions in the interior.

- Data from climate models are often scale limited due to coarse spatial resolution. In this case a single model data point might represent an area several degrees of latitude/longitude on a side and might entirely encompass the hydrological study area. This is also undesirable because local-scale climate heterogeneity is not reflected.

Poor coastal process understanding: Of less direct relevance to terrestrial hydrological modeling, but worth mentioning, is a poor understanding of coastal processes in general over the entire circum-Arctic domain. Coastal regions tend to be the "edge zones" for both oceanographic and land-surface models, and for theoretical studies, they tend to

fall into a jurisdictional "grey-zone" between terrestrial and marine researchers. Coastal processes represent the filter through which the results of terrestrial hydrological processes are passed before influencing the marine regime, and as such form an important component of the MMS general research mandate to achieve broader understanding of the north Alaska system.

Suggested Work in the Alaska Region

Improve the basic data record by establishing instrumentation initiatives for the following areas, in order of importance:

- The Brooks Range
- The interior regions of the North Slope
- The Alaskan Beaufort and Chukchi coasts

It is further suggested that such work be linked to the International Polar Year (IPY) initiative. During the previous IPY, efforts to begin monitoring large regions of low data availability were initiated. It is proposed that similar activities be conducted for the up-coming IPY, this time focusing on smaller areas. A project of simultaneous monitoring at multiple sites with a 10-year project horizon, such as is being proposed for IPY projects, would make substantial advances on the data gaps described above. Monitored parameters should also reflect needs of the hydrological community and include parameters not normally measured at a climate station, such as full energy balance components.

Climate model data should be downscaled to improve utility for the terrestrial hydrological modeling context. This includes:

- Predictive scenarios generated using the largest scale general circulation models, downscaled using
    a. Topoclimatic approach
    b. As boundary conditions to drive a regional climate model
- Current and hindcast (reanalysis) data generated using higher resolution forecast models, such as
    a. NCEP/NCAR Eta model (32 km resolution)
    b. Alfred Wegener Institute HIRHAM model

14

(20 km resolution)

The ultimate target scale for downscaling efforts should be on the order of 1 km, to be of use to the hydrological community.

- Accurate representation of precipitation for the Brooks Range/North Slope system must be established. In lieu of adequate observational data, a targeted regional modeling initiative should be undertaken for this region.

- Assess general circulation model output for the Alaska region, in terms of

  a. Internal consistency (i.e., model to model)

  b. Accuracy of representation (compared to observational data)

  Along with this an exploration of reasons for observed discrepancies should be undertaken. This will provide information on the following:

  a. It will indicate what aspects of the Alaska system present the greatest challenges for model representation. That is, what model sensitivities are activated by the Alaskan system

  b. Assessment of current performance will indicate which model(s) are best suited as a basis for future scenario prediction in the Alaskan region

- Establish an Alaska data clearing house. There are observational data sets that do exist; having them at one accessible portal would enhance future research efforts. Given the unique nature of Alaska in the U.S. arctic system, perhaps NSIDC could be approached to add an "Alaska" search term to their data sets.

- Evaluate the potential of satellite-derived data for providing climate fields relevant to hydrological modeling at the North Slope scale. Parameters could include surface and near-surface air temperature, snow water equivalent, or soil moisture content.

Theme 2: Hydrological Observations and Modeling (original records)

Discussion (See Appendix 3)

Scientific Objectives

- Combine USGS data, remote sensing of rivers and hydrologic modeling to produce continuous estimates of land surface discharge from the north slope into the Arctic Ocean

Recommendations

- Reestablish discontinued USGS gages

- Establish a 2–3 year intensive observation period for a North Slope region to compile multiple observational datasets for model evaluation

  a. Cover a gradient from the Brooks Range to the coastal region

  b. Wish list of desired variables

  c. Establish consistent gridded atmospheric dataset for all researchers

- Develop a web site to compile available data sets for the North Slope

- Require that all data generated by MMS-funded research be released after some time period

Scientific Objectives/Questions

- Better understanding of thermokarst occurrence and potential for increase in sediment and carbon

- Fluxes

- Groundwater dynamics, aufeis fields, and permafrost distribution

- Are better estimates of winter discharge possible through modeling?

Needs from Other Themes

- What range of temperature changes are actually important?

- Intelligent, physically-based scheme for downscaling course meteorology (e.g. EC-MWF) or interpolating station observations in data sparse regions

Areas of Streamflow Prediction

- Observation-based methods

  a. "Traditional" streamflow data collection

b. Remote-sensing based methods
- Hydrologic Modeling
  a. Small-scale, fully-distributed (topoflow)
  b. Macroscale, semi-physical (VIC, WAT-CLASS, SVAT)
  c. Intermediate Scale?
- Observational Directions and Needs
- Expanded gages for hydrologically interesting rivers
- Interest from the hydrological community
- Re-creating historical records through analysis of archived images
- High quality DEM

Modeling Needs – Data

- Meteorological Datasets
  a. Spatial patterns of T and P
  b. Vapor pressure and windspeed
  c. Radiation and cloud cover
- Spatial characterization data
  a. Soils, DEM, vegetation
- Calibration concerns
  a. More spatial datasets (SWE, soil moisture, ALD, river and lake break-up)
  b. Improved calibration: time to explore current state of models
  c. Storage terms

Modeling Needs – Algorithm

- Permafrost algorithms
  a. Varying levels of complexity exist
  b. Runoff dynamics (interflow, inter-hummock surface flow)
- Spatial variability in solar radiation and wind
- Shrub tundra melt dynamics
- Glaciers
- Snow albedo
- Snow damming/ice jams
- Water temperature prediction

Main Elements

- Reestablish USGS gages

- Cover a gradient from the Brooks Range to the coastal region
- Establish web site that provides links for data sets
- Combine different methods (RM, modeling, ground measurements)
- Scientific objectives: thermokarst, carbon cycle
- Groundwater dynamics, aufeis fields, and permafrost distribution

Theme 3: Priorities in Sea Ice, Oceanography, and Geochemistry (original records)

- Ocean/sea ice modeling community needs realistic high resolution, space and time, gridded datasets of the atmospheric forcing and freshwater inputs/fluxes, including error bars, std, rms
- Need independent validation data for models (atmosphere, ocean, sea ice)
- Resolve coastal geometry and coastal processes governing sea ice, land fast ice, coastal flow, and dynamics
- ~10 km hydrological model outputs to drive Arctic ice-ocean models in 3–5 year scope; 1–3 km for the North Slope for 10-year scope
- Coordinated field measurement and modeling studies: parallel efforts to maximize limited resources, use model guidance to choose ideal site for long-term/process studies
- Mackenzie runoff is important to local and large-scale ice/ocean circulation and water mass distribution
- Determine relative importance of North Slope vs. Mackenzie runoff impact on local ice-ocean dynamics; modeling sensitivity studies of the ocean dynamics response to freshwater inputs and pathways from the North Slope
- Freshwater dynamics in the upper 10 m coastal regime
- Prediction of effects of severe/single storms on coastal erosion, sediment transport, ecosystem variability, impact on humans, and pollutant dispersal
- Vertical transport/mixing, dense water forma-

tion due to atmospheric forcing – process studies and their relevance to large scale dynamics

- Remotely sensed data on surface ocean thermal fronts are useful for model

- Validation/improvements (12-year at 10 km data are already available, 1 km for 20 years possible

- Storm-induced coastal upwelling, changes in vertical structures of T&S

- Focused process studies of landfast ice, coastal currents, and density-driven circulation

- Improve/develop parameterizations of landfast ice in large scale ice-ocean models

- Measurements of freshwater flux through Bering Strait (long-term monitoring needed)

Executive Summary

Based on the working group recommendations listed above, a concise summary is drawn as follows:

Theme 1: Climate Variability and its Impacts

- Improve the basic data record by establishing observations (temperature, precipitation, wind, etc.) for the following areas, in order of importance:

  a) The Brooks Range

  b) The interior regions of the North Slope

  c) The Alaska Beaufort and Chukchi coasts linked to the International Polar Year initiative

- Climate model data should be downscaled to improve utility for the terrestrial hydrological modeling context. This includes

  a) Predictive scenarios generated using the largest scale general circulation models, downscaled using i) topoclimatic approach; ii) as boundary conditions, to drive a regional climate model

  b) Current and hindcast (reanalysis) data generated using higher resolution forecast models, such as i) NCEP/NCAR Eta model (32 km resolution);   ii) Alfred Wegener Institute HIRHAM model (20 km resolu-

tion)

  The ultimate target scale for downscaling efforts to be of use to the hydrological community should be on the order of 1 km

- Assess general circulation model output for the Alaska region, in terms of a) Internal consistency (i.e., model to model), and b) Accuracy of representation (compared to observational data)

- Establish an Alaska data clearing house. There are observational data sets that do exist; having them at one accessible portal would enhance future research efforts. Given the unique nature of Alaska in the U.S. arctic system, perhaps NSIDC could be approached to add an "Alaska" search term to their data sets

- Evaluate the potential of satellite-derived data for providing climate fields relevant to hydrological modeling at the North Slope scale. Parameters could include surface and near-surface air temperature, snow water equivalent, or soil moisture content

Theme 2: Hydrological Observation and Modeling

- Development of a fine-resolution (1–5 km) DEM-based hydrological model covering the entire North Slope from the Brooks Range to the coastal region (Fig. 10). The scientific objections are to understand

  a) thermokarst occurrence and potential for increase in sediment and carbon fluxes

  b) Groundwater dynamics, aufeis fields, and permafrost distribution

- Combine different methods (remote sensing, modeling, ground measurements). In addition, an intelligent, physically-based scheme for downscaling course meteorology (e.g. ECMWF) or interpolating station observations in data sparse regions should be developed

- Reestablish USGS gages on the North Slope

- Establish a web site that provides links for data sets

Theme 3: Sea Ice, Oceanography, and

17

Geochemistry

- High-resolution (1–5 km) ocean-sea ice models in the Chukchi-Beaufort seas should be developed under forcing of freshwater discharge (both point source/rivers and line source) derived from a high-resolution pan-North Slope DEM-based hydrological model.

ocean dynamics; modeling sensitivity studies of the ocean dynamics response to freshwater inputs and pathways from the North Slope

- Prediction of effects of severe/single storms on coastal erosion, sediment transport, eco-system variability, impact on humans, and pollutant dispersal, such as storm-induced

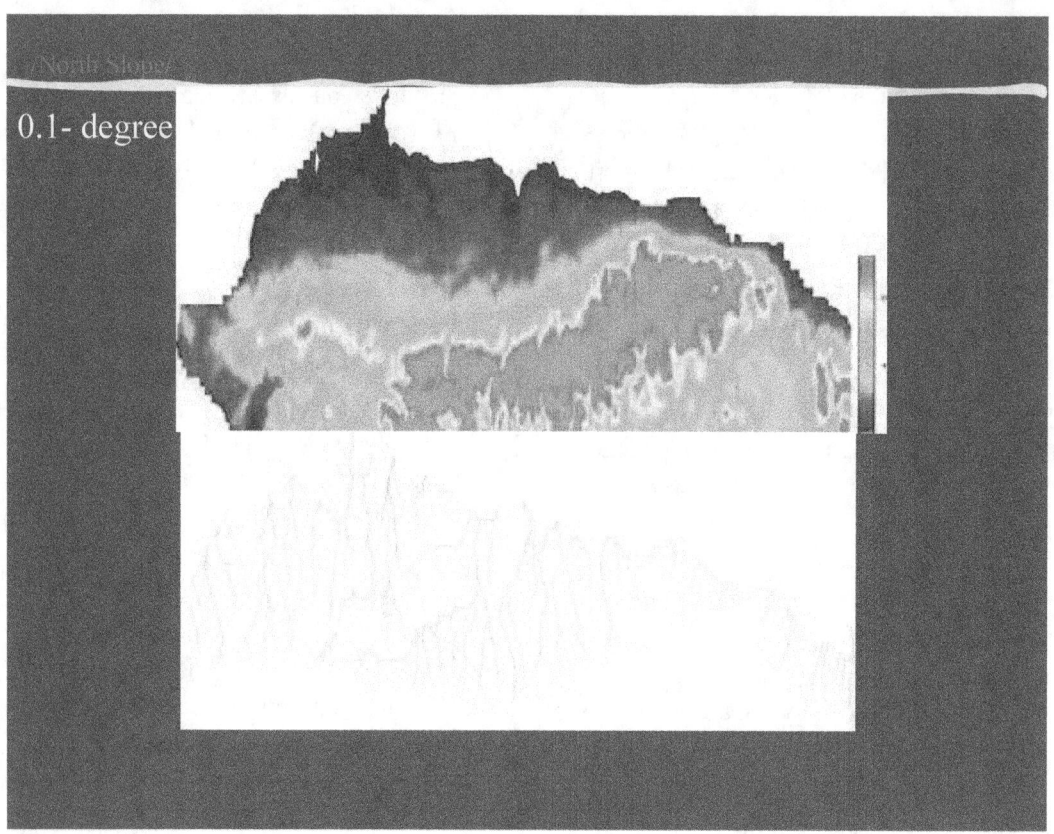

Figure 10. Proposed North Slope DEM-based hydrological model domain (upper panel) 0.1 degree DEM (topography); (lower panel) River network derived from the DEM (Courtesy of X. Ma).

Improve/develop parameterizations of land-fast ice in large scale ice-ocean models.

- Coordinated field measurement and modeling studies: parallel efforts to maximize limited resources, use model guidance to choose ideal site for long-term/process studies, such as focused process studies of landfast ice, coastal currents, fronts and density-driven circulation, and measurements of freshwater flux through Bering Strait.

- Determine relative importance of North Slope vs. Mackenzie runoff impact on local ice-

coastal upwelling, changes in vertical structures of T&S, and mixing

- Remotely sensed data on surface ocean thermal fronts for model validation/improvements, landfast ice, and multi-year sea ice

In summary, the workshop proposed an interdisciplinary (hydrology, meteorology, oceanography, sea ice, and geochemistry) integration/synthesis (I/S) study in the pan-North Slope (and Beaufort-Chukchi seas) region, an important research platform for oil and gas exploration and development. The proposed I/S in the pan-North Slope region can be linked to IPY 2007–2008.

The strategy of this I/S will combine modeling (ice-ocean, hydrological, and downscaling of atmospheric forcing) with field observations (river gages, meteorological measurements, satellite measurements, etc.). This can only be done through a strong project leadership (PI) with co-PIs in each component.

The approach of the I/S can be organized as a three-year project:

Year 1:

- Hydrological modeling
- Ice-ocean modeling with landfast ice and river runoff
- Atmospheric downscaling

Year 2:

- Hydrological model-data fusion studies
- Ice-ocean model-data fusion studies
- Atmospheric downscaling model-data fusion studies

Year 3:

- Couple the ice-ocean model to hydrological model forced by the downscaled atmospheric variables
- Project Leader organizes an I/S with a final report, and a possible special issue in a refereed journal or in a book

Acknowledgements

We sincerely thank the Coastal Marine Institute/University of Alaska Fairbanks, Minerals Management Service/U.S. Department of the Interior, and the International Arctic Research Center and Frontier Research System for Global Change for jointly sponsoring the workshop. We appreciate Vera Alexander and Syun Akasofu of the University of Alaska Fairbanks for their support and the workshop participants for their contributions.

References

Bowling, L.C., P.D. Lettenmaier and B.V. Matheussen 2000. Hydroclimatology of the Arctic drainage basin, p. 57–90. In E.L. Lewis, E.P. Jones, P. Lemke, T.D. Prowse and P. Wadhams [eds.], The Freshwater Budget of the Arctic Ocean. NATO Science Partnership Sub-Series 2, Vol. 70, Kluwer Academic Publishers, Dordrecht, The Netherlands.

Carmack, E.C. 2000. The Arctic Ocean's freshwater budgets: Sources, storage and export, p. 91–126. In E.L. Lewis, E.P. Jones, P. Lemke, T.D. Prowse, and P. Wadhams [eds.], The Freshwater Budget of the Arctic Ocean. NATO Science Partnership Sub-Series 2, Vol. 70, Kluwer Academic Publishers, Dordrecht, The Netherlands.

Eicken, H., I. Dmitrenko, K. Tyshko, A. Darovskikh, W. Dierking, U. Blahak, J. Groves, and H. Kassens. Submitted. Zonation of the Laptev Sea landfast ice cover and its importance in a frozen estuary. Submitted to Global Planet. Change.

Hinzman, L.D., M. Nolan, A. Carr, D.L. Kane, C.S. Benson, M. Sturm, G.E. Liston, J.P. McNamara, and D. Yang. 2000. Estimating snowpack distribution over a large arctic watershed, p. 13–18. In D.L. Kane [ed.], Water Resources in Extreme Environments. Proc. American Water Resources Association Conf., 1–3 May, 2000, Anchorage, Alaska.

Ikeda, M., J. Wang, and J.-P. Zhao. 2001. Hypersensitive decadal oscillations in the Arctic/subarctic climate. Geophys. Res. Lett. 28(7):1275–1278. doi: 10.1029/2000GL011773

Jin, M. and J. Wang. 2003. Implementation of an Ocean Circulation Model in GOA: A transition from SEA to GEM, Exxon Valdez Oil Spill Restoration Project Final Report, Chugach Development Corporation, Anchorage, Alaska.

Kane, D.L., R.E. Gieck, and L.D. Hinzman. 1997. Snowmelt modeling at small Alaskan Arctic Watershed. J. Hydrol. Eng. 2(4):204–210. doi: 10.1061/(ASCE)1084-0699(1997)2:4(204)

Kane, D.L., L.D. Hinzman, H. Yu, and D.J. Goering. 1996. The use of SAR satellite imagery to measure active layer moisture contents in arctic Alaska. Nordic Hydrol. 27:25–38.

Macdonald, R.W., E.C. Carmack, and D.W. Paton.

1999. Using the δ18° composition in landfast ice as a record of arctic estuarine processes. Mar. Chem. 65(1–2):3–24. doi: 10.1016/S0304-4203(99)00007-9

Macdonald, R.W., T. Harner, and J. Fyfe. 2005. Recent climate change in the Arctic and its impact on contaminant pathways and interpretation of temporal trend data. Sci. Total Environ. 342(1–3):5–86. doi: 10.1016/j.scitotenv.2004.12.059

Maslowski, W., B. Newton, P. Schlosser, A. Semtner, and D. Martinson. 2000. Modeling recent climate variability in the Arctic Ocean. Geophys. Res. Lett. 27(22):3743–3746. doi: 10.1029/1999GL011227

McNamara, J.P., D.L. Kane, and L.D. Hinzman. 1997. Hydrograph separations in an Arctic watershed using mixing model and graphical techniques. Water Resour. Res. 33(7):1707–1720. doi: 10.1029/97WR01033

McNamara, J.P., D.L. Kane, and L.D. Hinzman. 1998. An analysis of streamflow hydrology in the Kuparuk River Basin, Arctic Alaska: A nested watershed approach. J. Hydrol. 206(1–2):39–57. doi: 10.1016/S0022-1694(98)00083-3

Polyakov, I.V., R.V. Bekryaev, U.S. Bhatt, R.L. Colony, A.P. Maskshtas, and D. Walsh. 2003. Variability and trends of air temperature and pressure in the maritime Arctic, 1875–2000. J. Climate 16(12):2067–2077. doi: 10.1175/1520-0442(2003)016<2067:VATOAT>2.0.CO;2

Simmons, H.L. 1996. Estimation of Freshwater Runoff into Prince William Sound Using a Digital Elevation Model. M.S. Thesis, Univ. Alaska Fairbanks, 78 p.

Thompson, D.W.J. and J.M. Wallace. 1998. The Arctic Oscillation signature in the wintertime geopotential height and temperature fields. Geophys. Res. Lett. 25(9):1297–1300. doi: 10.1029/98GL00950

Walsh, J.E. V. Kattsov, D. Portis and V. Meleshko. 1998. Arctic precipitation and evaporation: Model results and observational estimates. J. Climate 11(1):72–87. doi: 10.1175/1520-0442(1998)011<0072:APAEMR>2.0.CO;2

Wang, J. and M. Ikeda. 2000. Arctic Oscillation and Arctic Sea-Ice Oscillation. Geophys. Res. Lett. 27(9):1287–1290. doi: 10.1029/1999GL002389

Wang, J. and M. Ikeda. 2001. Arctic sea-ice oscillation: Regional and seasonal perspectives. Ann. Glaciol. 33:481–492.

Wang, J., M. Ikeda, S. Zhang, and R. Gerdes. 2005. Linking the northern hemisphere sea-ice reduction trend and the quasi-decadal arctic sea ice oscillation. Clim. Dyn. 24(2–3):115–130. doi: 0.1007/s00382-004-0454-5

Wang, J., M. Jin, D.L. Musgrave, and M. Ikeda. 2004. A hydrological digital elevation model for freshwater discharge into the Gulf of Alaska. J. Geophys. Res. 109:C07009. doi: 10.1029/2002JC001430

Wang, J., Q. Liu, and M. Jin. 2002. A Nowcast/Forecast Model for the Beaufort Sea Ice–Ocean–Oil Spill System (NFM-BSIOS), p. 80–94. In University of Alaska Coastal Marine Institute Annual Report No. 8. OCS Study MMS 2002-001, University of Alaska Fairbanks and USDOI, MMS, Alaska OCS Region.

Wang, J., V. Patrick, J. Allen, S. Vaughan, C. Mooers, and M. Jin. 1999. Modeling seasonal ocean circulation of Prince William Sound, Alaska using freshwater of a line source, p. 55–66. In C.A. Brebbia and P. Anagnostopoulos [eds.], Coastal Engineering and Marina Development. Trans. on the Built Environment, vol. 43. WIT Press, Southampton, UK.

Weingartner, T.J. 1998. Circulation on the North Central Chukchi Sea shelf. Final Report. OCS Study MMS 98-0026, University of Alaska Coastal Marine Institute, University of Alaska Fairbanks and USDOI, MMS, Alaska OCS Region, 39 p.

Weingartner, T.J., D.J. Cavalieri, K. Aagaard, and Y. Sasaki. 1998. Circulation, dense water formation, and outflow on the northeast Chukchi shelf. J. Geophys. Res. 103(C4):7647–7662. doi: 10.1029/98JC00374

Wu, B., J. Wang, and J.E. Walsh. 2006. Dipole anomaly in the winter Arctic atmosphere and its association with sea ice motion. J. Climate

19(2):210–225. doi: 10.1175/JCLI3619.1

Yamamoto-Kawai, M., N. Tanaka, and S. Pivovarov. 2005. Freshwater and brine behaviors in the Arctic Ocean deduced from historical data of $\delta18^\circ$ and alkalinity (1929–2002 A.D.). J. Geophys. Res. 110:C10003. doi: 10.1029/2004JC002793

Yang, D., B. Goodison, J. Metcalfe, P. Louie, E. Elomaa, C. Hanson, V. Golubev, T. Gunther, J. Milkovic, and M. Lapin. 2001. Compatibility evaluation of national precipitation gage measurements. J. Geophys. Res. 106(D2):1481–1492. doi: 10.1029/2000JD900612

Yang, D., D.L. Kane, L. Hinzman, X. Zhang, T. Zhang, and H. Ye. 2002. Siberian Lena River hydrologic regime and recent change. J. Geophys. Res. 107(D23):4694. doi: 10.1029/2002JD002542

Appendix 1. Workshop Agenda.

Workshop Agenda

Hydrological Modeling of Freshwater Discharge from Alaska's Arctic Coast

October 7–8, 2004
International Arctic Research Center
Fairbanks, Alaska

Thursday, October 7 (IARC 401)

8:30–8:50 a.m.   Opening remarks, Introductions, Orientation to Fairbanks

Jia Wang	Workshop Chair
Paul Reichardt	Provost of UAF
Syun Akasofu	Director of IARC
Denis Wiesenburg	Dean of SFOS
Larry Merculieff	Alaska Native Science Commission

8:50–9:00 a.m.   "Workshop Expectations: MMS Perspective" by MMS Project
        Manager, Richard Prentki, Ph.D.

Theme 1 Chair: Larry Hinzman (Climate Variability and its Impacts)
(invited: 30 minutes, others: 25 minutes including 5 minutes questions; posters: 5 minutes)

9:00–11:05 a.m.

- •John Walsh: "Arctic Hydrological Variations in Global Climate Models" (invited)
- •Keith Echelmeyer: "Wastage of Brooks Range Glaciers: Relation to North Slope
        Hydrology"
- •David Atkinson: "Topoclimatic Modeling of Arctic Summer Screen-height Air
        Temperature"
- •Shusun Li: "Modeling and Measuring Spectral Bidirectional Reflectance Factor
        (BRF) of Snow: An Intercomparison Study"
- •Jessica Cherry: "Reconstructing Solid Precipitation in the Arctic with a Land Surface
        Hydrology Model"

11:05–11:20 a.m.   Coffee break

Theme 2 Chair: Steven Frenzel (Hydrological Observations and Modeling)

11:20–12:25 p.m.
- •Larry Hinzman: "Spatially Distributed Simulations of Permafrost Hydrology" (invited)
- •Laura Bowling: "Estimating the Freshwater Budget of High-latitude Land Surfaces"
- •W. Robert Bolton: "Simulation of the Influence of Discontinuous Permafrost On Hydrologic Processes" (5 mins, poster)
- •Kristin Susens: "Dynamic Hydrologic Processes on the Seward Peninsula" (5 mins, poster)

12:25: 12:40 p.m.   Group Photograph: Front steps of IARC Building

12:40–1:40 p.m.   Lunch: IARC 5th floor

1:40–2:00 p.m.   Personal Time. A computer is available in 401 to check your e-mail.

2:00–3:40 p.m.
- •David Bjerklie: "Development of a General Approach to Estimating Discharge in Alaskan Arctic Rivers from Remotely Sensed Information"
- •Robert Carlson: "Exploration of Hydrograph Analysis Techniques for Alaskan Arctic Coastal Watersheds"
- •Frank Seglenieks: "Hydrological Modeling of the Mackenzie Basin using WATFLOOD and WATCLASS in MAGS"
- •Stefan Pohl: "Hydrologic Modeling in the Tundra Region of NW Canada"

3:40–4:00 p.m.   Coffee break

4:00–5:50 p.m.
- •David Meyer: "USGS Streamflow Data Collection in Alaska"
- •Meibing Jin: "A Hydrological Digital Elevation Model for Freshwater Discharge into the Gulf of Alaska"
- •Xieyao Ma: "Hydrological Modeling in the Lena River Basin"
- •Daqing Yang: "Changes in Lena River Streamflow Hydrology: Human Impacts vs. Natural Variations" (5 minutes, poster)
  "Streamflow Response to Seasonal Snowcover Extent Changes in Large Siberian Watersheds" (5 minutes, poster)
- •Imke Schramm   "Hydrological Modeling of Imnavait Creek, Alaska's North Slope"

6:15 p.m.   Bus transportation departs for Pike's Landing Lodge (meet on front steps of IARC Building)

Friday, October 8

Theme 3 Chair: Nori Tanaka   (Sea Ice, Oceanography and Geochemistry)

8:30–9:20 a.m.
- •Hajo Eicken: "Dispersal of River Discharge in the Siberian Arctic and its Impact on the Sea-ice Environment: Lessons to be Learned for the North Slope Region?" (invited).
- •Igor Belkin: "Arctic Shelf Fronts and Their Relation to Freshwater Discharge"
- •Wieslaw Maslowski: "The Flow of Alaskan Coastal Current from the Gulf of Alaska to the Beaufort Sea – Challenges and Opportunities"

9:20–9:30 a.m.   Coffee break

9:30–10:45 a.m.
- •Robert Rember: "Riverine Transport and Dispersion of Freshwater, Suspended Sediment, Organic Carbon and Trace Metals in the coastal Beaufort Sea During the Spring Floods"
- •Michiyo Kawai: "Distribution of Freshwater Sources in the Western Arctic Ocean Derived From Chemical Tracers Oxygen Isotope Ratio and Alkalinity"
- •Jia Wang: "Intraseasonal and Interdecadal Variability of Arctic Freshwater and Heat Budget"

10:45–11:00 a.m.   Coffee break

10:45–12:30 p.m.   (35 minutes for each)
   Discussion of Theme 1:   Moderator: David Atkinson
   Discussion of Theme 2:   Moderator: Laura Bowling
   Discussion of Theme 3:   Moderator: Wieslaw Maslowski

12:30–1:40 p.m.   Lunch, IARC 5th floor

1:40–2:00 p.m.   Personal Time

2:00–3:45 p.m.   Breakout group meetings to finalize recommendations that each theme contributes:

		IARC Room
Discussion of Theme 1:	Rapporteur: David Atkinson	417
Discussion of Theme 2:	Rapporteur: Laura Bowling	401
Discussion of Theme 3:	Rapporteur: Wieslaw Maslowski	5th floor

3:45–4:00 p.m.   Coffee break

4:00–5:00 p.m.   Plenary session and summary by moderators of Themes 1–3 (Chair: Jia Wang)
David Atkinson   (15 minutes)
Laura Bowling   (15 minutes)
Wieslaw Maslowski   (15 minutes)

5:15 p.m.   Bus transportation departs for Pike's Landing Lodge
                            (meet on front steps of IARC Building)

6:30–9:30 p.m.   Workshop Dinner
                            Pike's Landing Lodge, Binkley Room

6:30–7:00 p.m.   Appetizers and No Host Bar

7:00–9:00 p.m.   Dinner

9:00–9:30 p.m.   Invited speaker–Dr. Doug Kane: "Future Direction of Arctic Hydrologic Research"

Appendix 2. Workshop Abstracts.

Workshop Abstracts

Theme 1: Climate Variability and its Impacts

Arctic Hydrological Variations in Global Climate Models
John E. Walsh

The simulated high-latitude precipitation in global coupled climate models generally exceeds the observational estimates, particularly over the terrestrial watersheds of the Arctic Ocean. The bias is larger in the coupled models than in uncoupled (atmosphere-only) models, and is strongest during the cold season, raising the possibility that the observational estimates may be too low. Multi-model means of the annual net surface moisture flux (P-E) are generally within the range of uncertainty of estimates of discharge from the rivers and streams of the Arctic terrestrial regions. The validity of the simulated values of evapotranspiration is not well known because of the large uncertainties in the observed values of E over the watershed scale.

The most carefully examined projections of changes in the 21st century in Arctic precipitation, evapotranspiration and river discharge are those in the soon-to-be-published Arctic Climate Impact Assessment. In general, the models project increases of precipitation over the Arctic. The areas of largest projected increase vary seasonally, from the North Pacific and North Atlantic storm tracks during winter to the inland Arctic terrestrial regions during summer. Depending on the scenario of increasing greenhouse gas concentrations, the projected increases of annual mean precipitation range from 5–15% (B2 scenario) to 10–30% (A2 scenario, 1% increase of CO^2) by the end of the 21st century. There is considerable disagreement among models concerning the projected changes of evapotranspiration, and even the sign of the projected change varies among models. There is a potentially important seasonality in the sense that the projected changes of P-E are generally smaller, and occasionally negative, over the major river basins during the warm season. The relative decrease of P-E during the summer is attributable to (1) an increase of E associated with the warming, and (2) the lengthening of the period with a snow-free surface and above-freezing temperatures in the upper soil layers. Despite the increase of summertime evapotranspiration, Arctic river discharge is projected to increase by 5–25% during the next century. The peak discharge occurs earlier in the year in response to the combination of earlier snowmelt, anticipated earlier river break-up, and increased summer evapotranspiration in the greenhouse scenarios.

Wastage of Brooks Range Glaciers: Relation to North Slope Hydrology
Keith Echelmeyer

We have measured surface elevations of about 100 glaciers throughout Alaska, NW Canada, and Washington using an airborne GPS/laser altimetry system and/or land-based profiling. Profiles were made in the early 1990's and many were repeated in 2000–2003, giving surface elevation, volume, and area changes over this time interval. These measurements were also compared to topographic maps made in the 1950s or 1970s to determine changes over these longer periods. Our findings indicate that most of these glaciers are thinning, decreasing in volume, and retreating. We have also found that changes in surface elevation are small at high elevations on any given glacier, but are quite large near the terminus.

The measured changes are generally larger during the period from the 1990s–2001 than those during the period 1950s–2001 or the period 1970s–2001. The wastage of these glaciers indicates a recent increase in temperature and/or a decrease in precipitation in Alaska and western Canada. The thinning rates of these 100 glaciers are significantly greater than previous estimates and are about twice the average thinning rate of the Greenland Ice Sheet over the recent period.

Included in our profiling measurements are eleven glaciers in the Brooks Range, all of which are located in the Arctic National Wildlife Refuge.

These glaciers are relatively small in area, but their temporal changes are an important component of the hydrology of the North Slope, including river discharges there. Their input complements the hydrologic input from aufeis, snowmelt, and spring-fed rivers. The changes of Brooks Range glaciers are also a key factor in assessing the ongoing climate change in arctic Alaska. However, these changes provide an insignificant contribution to sea level rise due to their small areal extent.

Topoclimatic Modeling of Arctic Summer Screen-height Air Temperature

David E. Atkinson

A DEM modeling solution is presented for climatological purposes, and could be applicable to hydrological issues either as an approach framework or to provide climate data at high spatial resolution as input to other hydrological models. Generally in arctic regions, weather observing stations are few and the spatial complexity of the region is high, which means temperature patterns are poorly resolved at the meso-scale. This issue was addressed over the Canadian Arctic Archipelago using a model to estimate surface air temperature. The effects on temperature due to site elevation and coastal proximity were selected for parameterization. The spatial basis is a 1 km resolution digital elevation model of the region (USGS GTOPO30 DEM) and the change in temperature with elevation was implemented in the model using derived environmental lapse rates. Advection effects were handled using resultant winds combined with air temperature above the ocean. Lapse rates and resultant wind estimates were obtained from rawinsonde ascents obtained at upper-air weather stations; however, multi-level modeled hindcast or forecast data could be utilized. Model results for 14-day runs were compared to observed data. The model was sensitive to steep surface inversions and to low-level warming. Sensitivity analyses were performed on the model to determine response to alterations in lapse rate calculation, sea surface temperature, and wind field generation. The model was most sensitive to the lapse rate calculation. The best results were obtained using a moderate lapse rate calculation, moderate wind field, and variable sea-surface temperature. This model will soon be implemented over Alaska and the western Canadian mainland arctic.

Modeling and Measuring Spectral Bidirectional Reflectance Factor (BRF) of Snow: An Intercomparison Study

Shusun Li and Xiaobing Zhou

Broadband albedo is a very important geophysical parameter in the Earth surface-atmosphere interaction in either global climate change or hydrological cycle and snowmelt runoff studies. To derive the broadband albedo accurately from satellite optical sensor observation at limited bands and at a single observation angle, the bidirectional reflectance factor (BRF) has to be quantitatively specified. In the present albedo derivation algorithms from the satellite radiance data, BRF is either modeled or observed. Questions may arise as to how well a BRF model can be in the broadband albedo derivation. To help answer such questions, we studied the performance of a snow surface BRF model for two specific cases under large solar zenith angles (65 and 85). We measured snow surface spectral directional reflectance under clear skies. The snow physical properties such as snow grain size and snow density at the same sites were also measured. In situ snow physical data are used to simulate the snow surface BRF and hemispherical directional reflectance factor (HDRF) through a multi-layered azimuth- and zenith-dependent plane parallel radiative transfer model. While the field measurements and BRF and HDRF simulations all reveal the forward-scattering nature of snow surface under large solar incidence angles, the BRF model results depict the strongest forward-scattering patterns under such solar zenith angles. Because the HDRF is simulated through coupling of surface BRF with radiative transfer in the atmosphere, the resulting HDRF patterns agree with the field measurements better than the simulated BRF does. The deviation of the simulated HDRF from field-based clear-sky directional reflectance (FCDR) is within 10% for the central (viewing zenith angle & lt; 45) and lateral sides of the viewing hemisphere. This level of agreement between the simulated HDRF and FCDR also implies that the simulated BRF model can provide remote sensing estimates of spectral albedo with an uncertainty of 10% for the same part of the viewing hemisphere. Further improvement in BRF model performance requires better handling of single scattering properties of snow grains, surface roughness, and atmospheric correction. Also, better procedures and techniques in field measurement are necessary for more accurate assessment of the performance of BRF models.

Reconstructing Solid Precipitation in the Arctic with a Land Surface Hydrology Model

Jessie Ellen Cherry

Much of the uncertainty in land-based Arctic freshwater estimates relates to the difficulty of measuring solid precipitation (Goodison et al. 1998). Precipitation gages that work well for liquid precipitation perform poorly for mixed and solid precipitation because the gage itself disrupts the boundary layer wind flow and causes snow to preferentially fall downwind from the gage (Sevruk 1998). Another problem in the Arctic is the paucity of gages (compared to mid-latitudes) which is compounded by creating gridded products for use in climate studies when there are only a few points of observation (Bowling et al. 2000). Such products are even more misleading when different countries and regions use different kinds of gages, each kind with a unique bias toward undercatch.

The goal of this proposal is to reconstruct a century-long record of solid precipitation in the Arctic by running the NASA Seasonal to Interannual Prediction Project (NSIPP) land surface hydrology model in an inverse mode (Ducharne et al. 2000, Koster et al. 2000). To this end, the model is run using observations of snow depth and surface air temperature to reconstruct the precipitation that must have fallen to produce the observed snow depth. Transport of snow by wind on the Arctic prairies may be as much as 75% (Pomeroy and Gray 1995) and sublimation induced by strong winds may account for losses to the atmosphere of nearly 30% (Pomeroy et al. 1997). For these reasons, the model includes compaction, surface sublimation, and blowing snow. This reconstruction is based on simple snow depth measurements using a ruler, with minimal instrumental error and little or no destructive influence on the snowpack. The snow depth record is quite long (back to 1890 in

some stations) and adds thousands of stations to the small number of precipitation gages in the Arctic (over 400 new stations in the Mackenzie catchment alone). By estimating the historical land-based solid precipitation in the Arctic, uncertainty in the Arctic freshwater budget associated with precipitation gages is significantly reduced.

The Reynolds Mountain station at Reynolds Creek Experimental Watershed (RCEW) in southwestern Idaho was chosen to calibrate and evaluate the method. Hourly measurements of all the relevant climate and hydrological variables for this study have been taken at RCEW since 1984 (Marks et al. 2001). Snow depth and snow water equivalent (SWE) are measured on several permanent snowcourses, twice monthly, and SWE is measured on an automatic snowpillow (pressure-based measurement of the weight of overlying snow) once hourly. RCEW was one site of the World Meteorological Organization's Solid Precipitation Intercomparison Project from 1987–1994, a time during which instrumental biases associated with several solid precipitation gages were carefully evaluated against the double fenced inter-comparison reference (DFIR), considered the least biased snow gage available. Transfer functions were then developed to adjust the gage data for known biases. These adjustments are applied to the precipitation observations for the present study.

First, the model is forced with corrected observed precipitation, surface temperature, surface pressure, vapor pressure, wind, incoming shortwave and longwave radiation. The simulated snow depth is then compared to observed snow depth (from cumulative corrected gages, pillows, and courses) to demonstrate the ability of the model to reproduce the observed snowpack. Then the model is run in an inverse mode to reconstruct precipitation. In this way, snowdepth observations and modeled snowpack physics are used to calculate how much precipitation must have occurred to produce the observed snow depth. Results from a pilot run show excellent agreement ($< 3\%$ yearly SWE) between NSIPP reconstructed precipitation and adjusted observed precipitation.

References

Armstrong, R. 2001. Historical Soviet Daily Snow Depth Version 2 (HSDSD). Boulder, CO, USA: National Snow and Ice Data Center. CD-ROM.

Bowling, L.C., D.P. Lettenmaier, and B.V. Matheussen. 2000. Hydroclimatology of the Arctic Drainage

Basin, in The Freshwater Budget of the Arctic Ocean. E.L. Lewis, ed. Dordrecht, Kluwer Academic Publishers, p. 57–90.

Brown, R.D., and R.O. Braaten. 1998. Spatial and temporal variability of Canadian monthly snow depths, 1946–1995. Atmosphere-Ocean, 36, 37–45.

Dickson, R.R. and J. Brown. 1994. The production of north Atlantic deep-water: sources, rates, and pathways. J. Geophys Res-Oceans, 99 (C6):12319–12341.

Ducharne, A, R.D. Koster, M.J. Suarez, et al. 2000. A catchment-based approach to modeling land surface processes in a general circulation model 2. Parameter estimation and model demonstration. J Geophys Res-Atmos, 105 (D20):24823–24838.

Goodison, B.E., H.L. Ferguson, and G.A. McKay. 1981. Measurement and Data Analysis, in Handbook of Snow. D.M. Gray and D.H. Male, eds. Ontario, Pergamon Press, pp. 191–274.

Goodison, B.E., P.Y.T. Louie, and D. Yang. 1998. WMO solid precipitation measurement intercomparison, final report. WMO/TD-No.872, WMO, Geneva, 212pp.

Hanover, N.H. Yang, D., and M.K. Woo. 1999. Representativeness of local snow data for large-scale hydrological investigations. Hydrological Processes, 13(2-13), 1977–1988.

Johnson, J.B. and G.L. Schaefer. 2002. The influence of thermal, hydrologic, and snow deformation mechanisms on snow water equivalent pressure sensor accuracy. Hydrol Process, 16 (18):3529–3542.

Koster, R.D., M.J. Suarez, A. Ducharne, et al. 2000. A catchment-based approach to modeling land surface processes in a general circulation model 1. Model structure. J Geophys Res-Atmos, 105 (D20):24809–24822.

Marks, D, K.R. Cooley, D.C. Robertson, et al. 2001. Long-term snow database, Reynolds Creek Experimental Watershed, Idaho, United States. Water Resour Res, 37 (11):2835–2838.

Meteorological Service of Canada (MSC), 2000. Canadian Daily Climate Data (CDCD). Downsview, Ontario, CANADA: National Archives and Data Management Branch. CD-ROM.

Pomeroy, J.W. and D.M. Gray. 1995. Snowcover Accumulation, Relocation and Management. NHRI Science Rep. No. 7, Saskatoon, 144 pp.

Pomeroy, J.W., P. Marsh, and D.M. Gray. 1997. Microphysics of Clouds and Precipitation, 2nd ed. Kluwer Academic Publishers, Dordrecht, 954 pp.

Serreze, M.C., J.E. Walsh, F.S. Chapin, et al. 2000. Observational evidence of recent change in the northern high latitude environment. Climatic Change, 46 (1–2):159–207.

Sevruk, B. 1998. Physics of precipitation gages, appendix in WMO solid precipitation measurement intercomparison, final report. WMO/TD-No.872, WMO, Geneva, 212 pp.

Work, R.A., H.J. Stockwell, T.G. Freeman, and R.T. Beaumont. 1965. Accuracy of field snow surveys, western United States, including Alaska. Tech. Rep. 163, U.S. Army Cold Reg. Res. Eng. Lab.

Theme 2: Hydrological Observations and Modeling

Spatially Distributed Simulations of Permafrost Hydrology

Larry Hinzman, W. Robert Bolton, Peter Prokein, Matt Nolan, and Kenji Yoshikawa

Permafrost is a strong factor in controlling many hydrologic processes including stream flow and soil moisture. Soil moisture, which displays a high spatial and temporal variability, is an important variable in understanding and predicting a large number of processes, including land-atmosphere interactions and permafrost aggradation/degradation. In order to understand and predict ecosystem

29

response to a changing climate and resulting feed-backs, it is critical to quantify the interaction of soil moisture and meteorology as a function of climatic processes, landscape type, and vegetation.

The primary goal of our research is to describe, simulate, and predict soil moisture dynamics and all other hydrologic processes everywhere throughout both sub-arctic and arctic watersheds. The model we are developing, TopoFlow, is being used as a tool to better understand the effects of vegetation and soil type, presence or absence of permafrost, the amount and timing of precipitation, and disturbance (such as wildfire) on soil moisture dynamics. Three small sub-basins of the Caribou-Poker Creeks Research Watershed (CP-CRW), located 48 km north of Fairbanks, Alaska (65° 10'N, 147° 30'W) and three nested watersheds in the Kuparuk Watershed (~68° 37'N, 149° 19'W) are the areas selected for study.

The primary control on local hydrological processes is dictated by the presence or absence of permafrost, but is also influenced by the thickness of the active layer and the total thickness of the underlying permafrost. As permafrost becomes thinner or decreases in areal extent, the interaction of surface and sub-permafrost ground water processes becomes more important. The inability of soil moisture to infiltrate to deeper groundwater zones due to ice rich permafrost maintains very wet soils in arctic regions. However, in the slightly warmer regions of the subarctic, the permafrost is thinner or discontinuous. In permafrost-free areas, surface soils can be quite dry as infiltration is not restricted, impacting ecosystem dynamics, fire frequency, and latent and sensible heat fluxes. Other hydrologic processes impacted by degrading permafrost include increased winter stream flows, decreased summer peak flows, changes in stream water chemistry, and other fluvial geomorphological processes. Hydrologic changes occurring in Alaska include drying of thermokarst ponds, increased active layer thickness, increasing importance of groundwater in the local water balance and differences in the surface energy balance.

Estimating the Freshwater Budget of High Latitude Land Surfaces

Laura C. Bowling, Jennifer Adam, Fengge Su, and Dennis P. Lettenmaier

Based on observations alone, we do not have the ability to close the water budget of the Alaskan North Slope, or to make predictions regarding its response to warmer temperatures. This presentation describes on-going research aimed at better estimating the North Slope regional water budget through the use of a large-scale, distributed hydrologic model, with a focus on the influence of surface water storage in wetlands and thaw ponds and sublimation from blowing snow. In the low-gradient watersheds of the coastal plain, permafrost contributes to the generation of extensive wetlands, ponds, and lakes in a semi-arid region of precipitation. In the Putuligayuk catchment, which drains into Prudhoe Bay, water balance calculations indicate that between 24 and 42% of snow melt water is not immediately available for runoff. This observed storage effect can be explained in large part by the excess of evapotranspiration over summer precipitation from open water areas, which results in a seasonal reduction in the extent of surface water of 58 to 73%. A lake and wetland algorithm added to the Variable Infiltration Capacity (VIC) macroscale hydrology model is able to simulate this seasonal reduction in wetland extent.

An algorithm that parameterizes the topographically induced sub-grid variability in wind speed, snow transport, and blowing snow sublimation was also designed for use within the VIC model. The algorithm is intended to provide consistent estimates of the relative influence of sublimation from blowing snow for continental-scale river basins, while balancing the land surface water and energy budgets. In addition to the standard land surface scheme inputs, the model requires specification of the standard deviation of terrain slope, the mean fetch, and the lag one autocorrelation of terrain gradients. Model predictions of end-of-season snow water equivalent (SWE) compare favorably with observations for Imnavait Creek and other sites throughout the Kuparuk River basin on the Alaskan North Slope. Annual average sublimation from blowing snow predicted by the model for the Kuparuk River watershed varies from 47 mm in the foothills of the Brooks Range to approximately 31 mm on the Arctic coastal plain; sublimation was primarily controlled by topographic limitations on fetch in the foothills and by precipitation and vapor pressure on the coastal plain.

The results from these studies reveal a number of ongoing scientific challenges to accurately predict regional runoff. These include observational shortcomings associated with solid precipitation, relative humidity, and wind speed, as well as modeling challenges associated with the role of recharge to upland tundra areas and the pathways of water exchange between the tundra and surface water networks. These will be discussed within the context of strategies for prediction of runoff from the entire North Slope domain.

Simulation of the Influence of Discontinuous Permafrost on Hydrologic Processes

W. Robert Bolton and Larry Hinzman

In the sub-arctic environment, permafrost is a strong factor in controlling many hydrologic processes including stream flow and soil moisture. Soil moisture, which displays a high spatial and temporal variability, is important in understanding and predicting a large number of processes, including land-atmosphere interactions and permafrost aggradation/degradation. In order to understand and predict ecosystem response to a changing climate and resulting feedbacks, it is critical to quantify the interaction of soil moisture and meteorology as a function of climatic processes, landscape type, and vegetation.

The primary goal of our research is to describe, simulate, and predict soil moisture dynamics and all other hydrologic processes everywhere throughout a sub-arctic watershed. The model we are developing, TopoFlow, is being used as a tool to better understand the effects of vegetation and soil type, presence or absence of permafrost, the amount and timing of precipitation, and disturbance (such as wildfire) on soil moisture dynamics. Three small sub-basins of the Caribou-Poker Creeks Research Watershed (CPCRW), located 48 km north of Fairbanks, Alaska (65° 10'N, 147° 30'W), are the areas selected for study. These small sub-basins, which are underlain with approximately 3, 19, and 53% permafrost, are simulated to explore differences in permafrost versus non-permafrost areas.

The primary control on local hydrological processes is dictated by the presence or absence of permafrost, but is also influenced by the thickness of the active layer and the total thickness of the underlying permafrost. As permafrost becomes thinner or decreases in areal extent, the interaction of surface and sub-permafrost ground water processes becomes more important. The inability of soil moisture to infiltrate to deeper groundwater zones due to ice-rich permafrost maintains very wet soils in arctic regions. However, in the slightly warmer regions of the subarctic, the permafrost is thinner or discontinuous. In permafrost-free areas, surface soils can be quite dry as infiltration is not restricted, impacting ecosystem dynamics, fire frequency, and latent and sensible heat fluxes. Other hydrologic processes impacted by degrading permafrost include increased winter stream flows, decreased summer peak flows, changes in stream water chemistry, and other fluvial geomorphological processes. Hydrologic changes occurring in Alaska include drying of thermokarst ponds, increased active layer thickness, increasing importance of groundwater in the local water balance, and differences in the surface energy balance.

Dynamic Hydrologic Processes on the Seward Peninsula

Kristin Susens and Larry Hinzman

The purpose of this project is to contribute to a more complete understanding of hydrologic and meteorological processes as impacted by varying proportions of permafrost due to climate change. We have been studying the hydrologic processes occurring in nested watersheds of the Kuparuk river basin on the North Slope of Alaska, U.S.A. since 1985. This project compares and contrasts watersheds in a slightly warmer region of the Arctic, the Seward Peninsula. The hydrology of the Seward Peninsula is simulated using a spatially distributed hydrologic model, TopoFlow, which was developed in our laboratory and verified on watersheds in the Interior and the North Slope of Alaska. Complementary measurements of all the important components of the surface water and energy balances are currently being collected in two watersheds on the Seward Peninsula, Kuzitrin River near Kougarok (drainage area ~4450 km^2)

and Snake River near Nome (~220 km^2). Water balance computations include the measurements or computations of precipitation, evapotranspiration, runoff, and storage change in snow, ice, groundwater, and soil water. These hydrological and meteorological elements vary spatially and temporally, and most water balance computations will deal with the computations of time-average. On large time and space scales, subpermafrost groundwater also becomes an important factor. With projected increases in surface temperature and decreases in surface moisture levels, the active layer thickness will probably increase and permafrost area extent will decrease, leading to subtle but predictable ecosystem responses such as vegetation changes. Permafrost in arctic regions exerts a significant influence upon hydrologic and ecosystem dynamics through controls on vegetation and drainage. In relatively flat areas where the frozen layer is near the surface, the soil moisture contents are usually quite high. These areas have relatively high evapotranspiration and sensible heat transfer, and a low conductive heat transfer due to the insulative properties of thick organic soils. The climax vegetative species and soil forming processes are dominantly controlled by the closely coupled permafrost and hydrologic conditions. As permafrost degrades, the soil moisture holding capacity increases, soil drainage improves and moisture is no longer held near the surface but percolates to deeper reservoirs. As permafrost becomes thinner or absent, groundwater contributions from springs become more important.

Development of a General Approach to Estimating Discharge in Alaskan Arctic Rivers from Remotely Sensed Information

David Bjerklie

Previous studies suggest that remotely-sensed river hydraulic data could be used to directly estimate the discharge of rivers in specific reaches with typical accuracies within plus or minus 50%, and a mean accuracy within 10%. With limited ground information and appropriate regional river classification schemes, this accuracy can likely be improved. The advantage of using remote sensing is that it has the capability to provide information over large areas including those that are difficult to access. Thus, if site specific discharge ratings can be developed from hydraulic information observed from remote platforms, discharge dynamics in rivers with little or no historical discharge records could be estimated from the historic record of remote imagery and other remote data sources.

The water surface width (estimated from water surface area), channel slope, and mean channel width (estimated from channel surface area) can all be obtained from existing remote sources, including topographic information, visible spectrum satellite and aerial images, and synthetic aperture radar (SAR) images. In some cases, the surface velocity of rivers can also be observed remotely using synthetic aperture radar. At least since the late 1970's, satellite and aerial imagery of the Alaskan arctic have been routinely collected and archived. Although a continuous time series of imagery for a specific river reach would generally not be available, a relatively long sequence of remotely sensed river widths could be assembled for analysis. These data combined with historic stream gage records for the Alaska arctic and sub-arctic would provide the necessary data to develop, test, and calibrate a general approach to estimating river discharge from remote data sources.

Unique hydrologic issues that would be addressed include the effects of ice and ice damming, and frozen channel bottoms. These issues would be addressed by using an unsteady flow model coupled with a general resistance equation that is calibrated using the Froude number. The general approach is based on new formulations of general flow-resistance equation(s) that do not require site-specific estimates of flow resistance as input. Instead, resistance is explained to the maximum extent possible by measurable hydraulic variables and channel morphology. The study will develop general relationships between observable hydraulic variables (width, slope) and flow resistance from existing regional discharge data (USGS NWIS data for Alaska), and incorporate these data into an unsteady flow model developed from channel geometry information.

Exploration of Hydrograph Analysis Techniques for Alaskan Arctic Coastal Watersheds

Robert F. Carlson

32

Analysis of the daily streamflow hydrograph records of Alaskan arctic coast streams is a valuable, but underutilized, tool for understanding freshwater discharge. At the present time, most studies refer to only mean annual discharge or, perhaps, the single daily peak flow for the season. Yet, classic streamflow analysis provides a rich store of information for understanding modeling efforts of freshwater discharge. The USGS lists 16 stream gage sites with 8 sites of more than one year of record in the North Slope region. A typical analysis sequence will yield the following information–volume and seasonal pattern of groundwater flow; dates of break-up and freeze-up; volume and pattern of the spring breakup flow; number, volume, peak, and pattern of summer rainstorms; calculation of flow recession values of groundwater and surface run-off; and volume and pattern of winter flow (if the data is available). The annual streamflow pattern can also be subject to model-free time series analysis including auto regressive-integrated-moving average (ARIMA) analysis and singular spectrum analysis (SSA). These techniques may generate parameters that are instructive for understanding the nature of watershed runoff patterns within a season and from year to year. Finally, linear reservoir conceptual models, through numerical inversion with the streamflow data, can identify watershed parameters and inputs. These techniques are illustrated for several of the long-term streamflow records in the Arctic coastal region.

Hydrological Modeling of the Mackenzie Basin Using WATFLOOD and WATCLASS in MAGS

F. Seglenieks and E.D. Soulis

The objective of the Mackenzie Basin GEWEX Study (MAGS) is to understand the water and energy balance for the Mackenzie river basin. In such a data sparse area, modeling plays an important role by providing a framework for integration of observations into a consistent description of the budgets. The particular challenges of the Mackenzie are that the database is extremely limited, and the processes are poorly understood for the northern domains. Therefore the modeling effort must be as comprehensive as possible, involving atmospheric and hydrologic models that are tightly integrated and use all available data.

The challenge for the Mackenzie is to conduct modeling in a data sparse environment. There are approximately 82 operational streamgages in the 1.7 million square kilometer basin and a similar number of synoptic weather stations. Although not typical of the developed world, this low network density is characteristic of much of the globe. This gives special importance to work in the Mackenzie, as the techniques developed will be more appropriate globally than models developed in data rich environments. An extensive database has been developed to support the modeling program.

Another challenge is the northern climate of the watershed. Although many existing hydrologic models have winter components, the parameterizations are usually not developed well enough to accommodate the extreme northern conditions in the Mackenzie. Also, physiographic considerations such as permafrost, frozen soils, snow sublimation, and snow redistribution are rarely incorporated in most hydrological models. There are major problems when models are transposed from temperate climates and are applied to northern environments.

The modeling system is built in stages by combining two well-established Canadian codes: WATFLOOD and CLASS. WATFLOOD has a well-developed routing scheme and provides a solid connection to the streamflow records. CLASS, the Canadian Land Surface Scheme, pays great attention to the vertical and water energy budget and has an appropriate interface to atmospheric models. The resulting code, WATCLASS, combines these strengths.

WATFLOOD was developed at the University of Waterloo starting in 1973 as a flood forecasting model. The WATFLOOD model divides a watershed into a number of Grouped Response Units (GRU) and discretizes the basins into a series of square grids. The surface water budget is computed for each GRU within a grid square and infiltrated using the well-known Green-Ampt approach. When the infiltration capacity is exceeded by the water supply, and the depression storage has been satisfied, the model then computes overland flow from the Manning equation. Infiltrated water is stored in a soil reservoir referred to as the Upper Zone Storage (UZS). Water within this layer percolates downward or is exfiltrated to nearby water-courses using simple storage-discharge relationships.

The development of CLASS began in 1987 in response to the perceived need for second-generation land surface modeling within the Canadian GCM. In CLASS, land cover is dealt with using a patched landcover, or mosaic approach. Each modeled grid cell can have up to four subareas, representing bare soil, vegetation-covered, snow-covered, and snow-and-vegetation covered "patches" of the landscape. Inputs of meteorological variables at the bottom of the atmosphere are used to drive the energy and moisture balances for each of the subareas, and the resulting fluxes to the atmosphere are passed back to the host atmospheric model. The surface energy balance is solved for each subarea by expressing the various fluxes as functions of a single unknown, the surface temperature (of the vegetation, snow or soil as appropriate), and then solving iteratively.

The coupling of WATFLOOD and CLASS was begun in 1997, however the process was not straightforward and it has taken many years to fully integrate the models. Both models are land-covered based, and have similar land cover categories but the treatments of mixed covers are significantly different. For example, each blends different state variables within an element and many of the parametizations are slightly different. The combined model was constructed using CLASS for the vertical processes and WATFLOOD for the horizontal process. In the WATCLASS model, the generation of runoff is assigned to CLASS and the routing is carried out by WATFLOOD.

Use of distributed hydrologic models requires a detailed description of topography and sub-basin boundaries for a watershed. These were compiled from the USGS GTOPO30 digital terrain model, with the basin being divided into a 20 km polar-stereographic grid with 4700 elements. These models also require land cover information for the watershed. A land cover product developed by the Canada Center for Remote Sensing (CCRS) proved to be the most accurate in a previous study done for MAGS. The thirty-one land classes of the CCRS land-cover product were consolidated into 7 land classes: Barren, Coniferous Forest, Deciduous Forest, Cropland, Glacier, Wetland, and Water (Figure 1).

WATFLOOD and WATCLASS require gridded surface meteorological data to drive their hydrologic calculations. Data for this purpose traditionally have been derived from interpolated measured station data and measured weather radar; however, more recently Global Circulation Model (GCM) and Numerical Weather Prediction (NWP) archive data have been used successfully. For this study, data were obtained from two models operated by the Canadian Meteorological Centre; the Regional Finite Element (RFE) model and the Global Environmental Multiscale (GEM) model. Output from the gridded forecast portion of the archive was used as the forcing data set for WATFLOOD and WATCLASS for the period of 1994–2001. Because of the inherently poor predictability of precipitation, the gridded precipitation data obtained from the NWP models were adjusted in an attempt to match observations from the climate network.

In order to improve the streamflows that were simulated, the parameter sets were calibrated for the Mackenzie basin. To begin, an initial parameter set was used that has been derived by running WATFLOOD and WATCLASS on many different watersheds both within Canada and around the world. This initial parameter set was then calibrated for two years (1995–1996) using measured flows from the Liard river basin. The Liard River was chosen as it is the largest watershed in the basin that does not have regulated flows or large lakes. To calibrate the model, the parameters were adjusted, within limits, to minimize the square of the difference between the measured and simulated flows. This calibrated parameter set was then used to run the models for the rest of the time period over the entire basin. Apart from those two years on the Liard river basin, all other simulated streamflows can be considered an evaluation (or validation) of the parameter set. Figures 1 and 2 show simulated and measured streamflows at various locations within the Mackenzie basin using WATFLOOD and WATCLASS after calibration.

Along with streamflows, the models also calculate the components of the basin's water budget: precipitation, evaporation, and runoff. The difference between the incoming precipitation and the combined evaporation and runoff can be considered the year-over-year change in storage. Tables 1 and 2 show the water budget calculated using both the WATFLOOD and WATCLASS models.

The WATFLOOD and WATCLASS streamflow results show good overall agreement with the measured values. In general, both the timing and volume of the peak flows are well represented. The best results are for the Liard River where the parameter calibration was performed for two years. However, there are definitely improvements that can be made to the simulated flows of the Mackenzie River at Arctic Red River. Most of the flow at this station is dependent on the outflow of Great Slave Lake; hence improvement in the simulated streamflow will require an updated stage-discharge relationship for the outlet of the lake. There are also problems with too much flow volume at the Athabasca River station.

In general there is good agreement between the water budgets of the two models; the difference in the average yearly change in storage is less than 1% of the incoming precipitation. The WATCLASS model shows higher evaporation and less runoff than the WATFLOOD model. Unfortunately, the values of the water budget components are difficult to measure, and as a result, other sources are being investigated to obtain independent measures of these components. These include output from other models, indirect measurements using remote sensing, and direct measurements made on a small scale. In the future these will be used to verify the components of the water budget and may lead to changes in the models in order to produce more realistic values.

Future modeling efforts will focus on the interaction of soil moisture and transpiration from vegetation, optimization of land-surface parameters

Table 1. Water balance for seven water years using WATFLOOD (all values in mm of water).

Water Year	Precipitation	Evaporation	Hydrologic P-E	Local Runoff	Delta Storage
1994-1995	368.3	182.5	185.8	188.6	-2.8
1995-1996	460.1	188.2	272.0	248.8	23.2
1996-1997	472.2	205.3	267.0	265.1	1.8
1997-1998	370.4	185.6	184.8	202.9	-18.1
1998-1999	427.1	147.8	279.2	260.9	18.4
1999-2000	444.9	154.8	290.2	280.3	9.9
2000-2001	424.6	143.3	281.2	291.4	-10.1
Average	423.9	172.5	251.4	248.3	3.2

Table 2. Water balance for seven water years using WATCLASS (all values in mm of water).

Water Year	Precipitation	Evaporation	Hydrologic P-E	Local Runoff	Delta Storage
1994-1995	358.5	204.1	154.4	173.6	-19.2
1995-1996	462.8	186.5	276.3	238.5	37.8
1996-1997	474.9	180.8	294.0	286.5	7.5
1997-1998	367.3	208.4	158.9	181.6	-22.8
1998-1999	425.9	180.8	245.1	243.5	1.6
1999-2000	436.2	171.2	265.1	246.5	18.5
2000-2001	420.2	167.4	252.8	259.2	-6.4
Average	426.1	185.3	240.8	239.5	-0.3

using hydrographs, and the parameterization of snow processes including permafrost, frozen soil, snow sublimation, and snow redistribution.

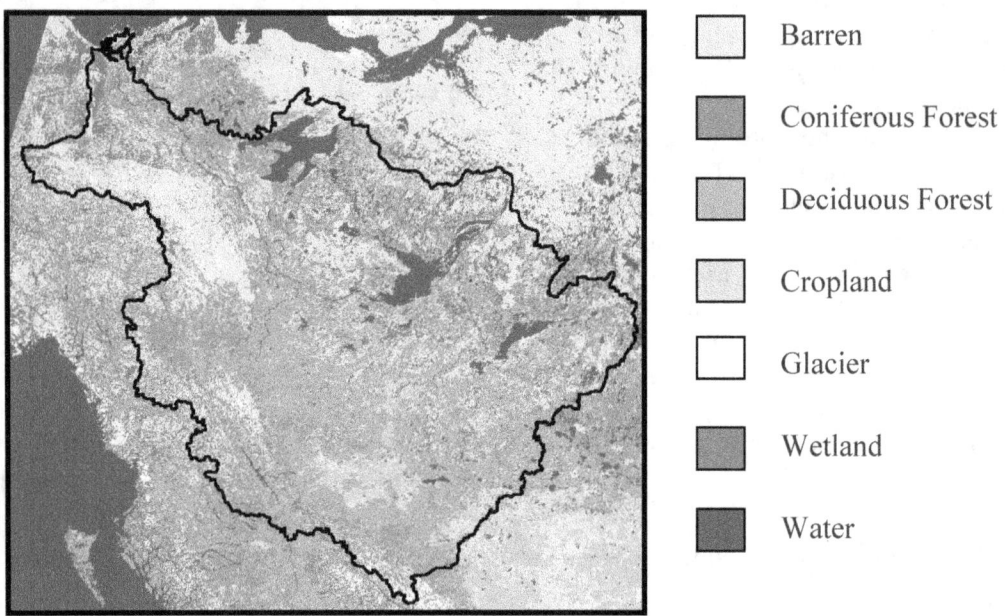

Figure 1. Land cover map for the Mackenzie basin derived from the Canada Centre for Remote Sensing.

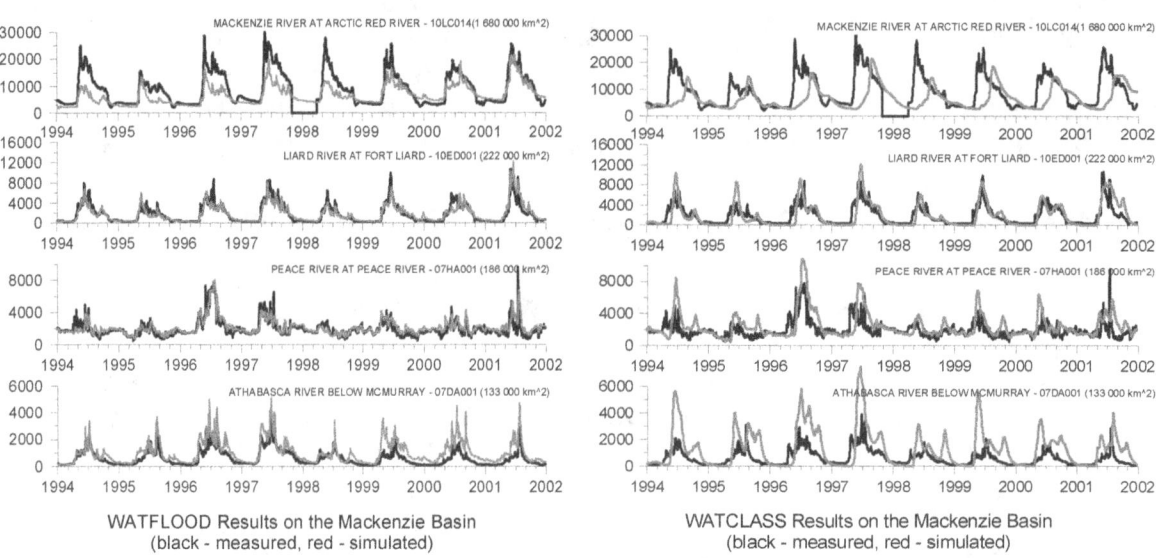

Figure 2. WATFLOOD and WATCLASS results on the Mackenzie basin for the years 1994–2001. The gage on the Mackenzie River at Arctic Red River (top hydrograph) has the largest drainage area while the other three hydrographs represent the three main sub-basins of the Mackenzie River. Note that the Peace River contains a major hydroelectric dam and thus a majority of its flow is regulated.

Hydrologic Modeling in the Tundra Region of NW Canada

S. Pohl, P. Marsh, A. Pietroniro, B. Davison, C. Onclin, and M. Russell

This paper will consider various process and hydrologic modeling studies being carried out in NW Canada. These studies have utilized a variety of hydrologic models including WATFLOOD and WATCLASS and will utilize TopoFlow in the near future. This paper will concentrate on results to date and the physical process studies carried out in support of model development. Results reported in this paper are for a small research basin (less than 100 km^2), but this research is in support of a variety of larger scale modeling efforts, including: the Mackenzie GEWEX Study (MAGS); estimating flow from ungaged areas; and various climate change studies for example.

The hydrology land-surface scheme WATCLASS has been tested in order to simulate spring snowmelt runoff in Trail Valley Creek (TVC) – a small arctic basin dominated by open tundra and shrub tundra vegetation. TVC enters the Beaufort Sea east of the Mackenzie Delta. WATCLASS calculates snowmelt rates from a full surface energy balance, and a three layer soil model is used to simulate the infiltration into and the exchange of heat and moisture within the ground. The generated meltwater is delivered to the stream channel network by overland flow, interflow, and baseflow and subsequently routed out of the catchment. Five spring snowmelt periods with a variety of initial end-of-winter snow cover and melt conditions were simulated and compared against observed runoff data. A main component of this stage of model validation considered the models ability to simulate spatially variable snow covered area (SCA) within the basin. Variable snow covered area is believed to be an important process in controlling both the fluxes of energy between the landsurface and atmosphere, and snowmelt runoff. The ability of WATCLASS to model spatially variable snow cover was carried out by comparing model predictions to remotely sensed SCA.

Results show that WATCLASS was able to fairly accurately predict runoff volumes, as well as timing of snowmelt and meltwater runoff, for open tundra. However, the model underestimated melt in the energetically more complex shrub tundra areas of the basin. This was not a major issue for the study basin, but would be for areas with larger areas of shrub tundra. This is especially a problem for climate change studies, as the area of shrub tundra is expected to increase under various future climate scenarios. Furthermore, the large observed spatial variability of the modeled SCA were not captured well at the 1 km model resolution. Recommendations to improve model performance in arctic basins include: a more realistic implementation of the gradual deepening of the thawed layer during the spring to improve runoff predictions, and the use of topographic information in the definition of land cover classes for the grouped response unit (GRU) approach employed by the model to handle subgrid variability. This would include a better prediction of the variability of both snow water equivalent (SWE) and energy fluxes controlling snowmelt rates.

Subsequent research has considered the relative importance of variable SWE vs. variable energy fluxes, including both solar radiation and turbulent fluxes driven by spatially variable wind speed, in low-relief tundra basins. Small scale process models were developed to consider the spatial variability in solar radiation and latent/sensible heat flux during spring melt (controlled both by spatially variable wind speed and small scale advection of sensible heat from the snow-free to snow-covered patches). These model results are able to accurately predict both snow-covered area and the distribution of patches when compared to remote sensing images of snow covered area, and clearly demonstrate the relative importance of various processes in controlling the development of a patchy snow cover. In addition, recent work has demonstrated the role of shrubs in affecting snow melt. Ongoing work is concentrating on including these small scale processes into WATCLASS in order to better estimate both the exchange of energy between the snow covered terrain and the atmosphere, and runoff for both small and large scale model applications.

USGS Streamflow Data Collection in Alaska

David F. Meyer

The U.S. Geological Survey (USGS) has collected streamflow information in Alaska since 1906.

However, continuous records have been collected only since the 1970s. The stream gaging network in Alaska, and specifically in the Arctic, is sparse relative to the conterminous United States. The number of daily discharge stations in Alaska equates to about 1 station for every 5,100 square miles. In the "lower 48", there is about one station for every 400 square miles. On the North Slope, there have been only 15 continuous stream gages since streamflow data collection began, and only 6 are active today, about one for every 10,000 square miles. In a recently completed flood frequency study of Alaska rivers, only 24 gages with 10 or more years of peak flow record could be used for the arctic region of Alaska that includes drainages to the Arctic Ocean, and Norton and Kotzebue Sounds.

Currently, 122 continuous streamflow gaging stations and 70 partial-record gages are operating in Alaska. Stage and discharge data from 90 of these gages, as well as most historical data, are accessible in real-time through the Internet. These data are collected, reviewed, and archived to nationally consistent, documented standards. At many of these gages, rainfall and water temperature are also collected and transmitted. Most are operated year round, though determination of streamflow under ice is possible only by direct discharge measurement. Continuous streamflow must be estimated between visits.

Stream gages are funded through the USGS National Streamflow Information Program, which is a direct Congressional appropriation, through interagency agreements with other Federal Agencies, including the Corps of Engineers, Forest Service, and Bureau of Land Management, and through cooperative agreements with state and local agencies and Native Tribal Councils. In cases where private entities need hydrologic data that is also in the National interest, funding is frequently provided by various state agencies, which in turn sign agreements with those private entities. In many cases, USGS matches as much as 50% of the funding provided by state and local agencies through the USGS Cooperative Program. Funding for stream gaging, both direct and through the Cooperative Program has been declining over the past few years.

New techniques promise more effective and safer data collection. Non-contact stream stage measuring currently is being tested, and will provide more reliable records during breakup, when the Arctic rivers normally peak. Acoustic Doppler current profiling to measure stream discharge is widespread, and can provide quicker, more accurate measurements of stream discharge. Helicopter-mounted ground-penetrating radar, coupled with Doppler radar, shows promise for making non-contact discharge measurements possible, even during periods when ice flow precludes more routine streamflow measurement. However, access to remote sites remains expensive and time-consuming. Even with these new techniques, financial resources will likely limit hydrologic data coverage in remote areas.

A Hydrological Digital Elevation Model for Freshwater Discharge into the Gulf of Alaska

Jia Wang, Meibing Jin, David L. Musgrave, and Moto Ikeda

Freshwater discharge into the Gulf of Alaska (GOA) has an important effect on coastal circulation. In order to incorporate freshwater discharge into a 3-D ocean circulation model with both point sources (big rivers) and line sources (gridded coastlines), a digital elevation model (DEM) was developed to simulate freshwater discharge into GOA under forcing of daily air temperature and precipitation data from NCEP/NCAR reanalysis during 1958–1998. This GOA-DEM includes glacier, snow storage, and melting processes. Coastal freshwater discharge into GOA displays a very strong seasonal cycle and interannual variability. The comparison of simulated runoff with gaged (observed) river discharge was conducted for two major rivers (Copper River and Susitna River), showing a good agreement on seasonal cycle and interannual variability. The simulated annual mean of the total freshwater discharge into GOA ranges from 19,000 to 31,000 m^3s^{-1} (with a mean of 23,100 m^3s^{-1}) for the period of 1958–1998. In the winter season (November to April), precipitation is mainly stored as snow, and freshwater discharge remains as a small base flow with some occasional changes due to short-term temperature increase. Freshwater discharge starts to rise sharply from May due to increasing precipitation and above-freezing temperatures, and remains high from June through September because of snow melt and some melting glaciers. In October, the discharge decreases rapidly, to a basic flow in December as the temperature drops below the freezing point.

Freshwater discharge into GOA can be divided into the point sources (big rivers) and the line sources (ungaged numerous small streams and creeks due to melting of snow and glaciers). The model shows that five major rivers (point sources) account for about 50.6% of the total drainage areas, while the line source accounts for 49.4% of the drainage area. However, our new finding is that the point sources only account for 26%, while the line sources contribute 74% to the total runoff. Thus, discharge from line sources (ungaged small rivers, streams, and creeks) is 2.8 times greater than the point sources (five large rivers).

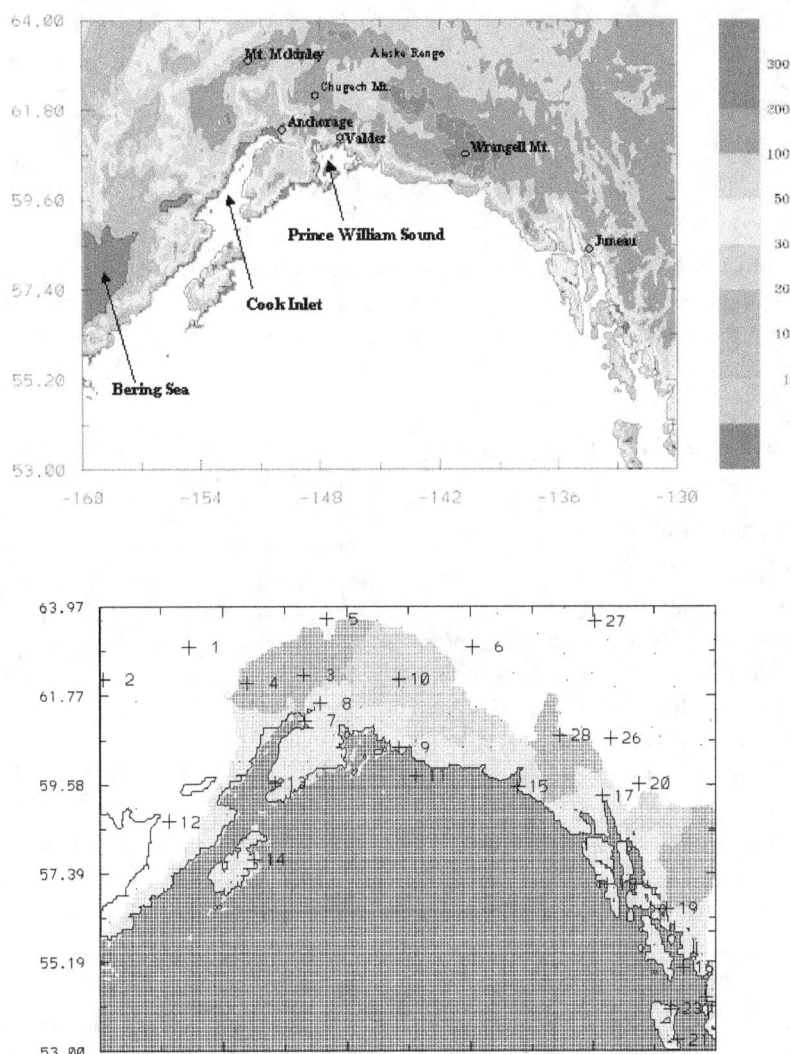

Figure 1. Elevation in the model study area (top panel), and the watershed of the line source (in yellow) and five big rivers (in colors) (bottom panel), which are named (from left to right) Susitna, Copper, Alsek, Taku, and Stikine rivers. The "+" signs denote the NCDC stations available in the study region. Note that these rivers have interior drainages, while the line source has coastal drainages.

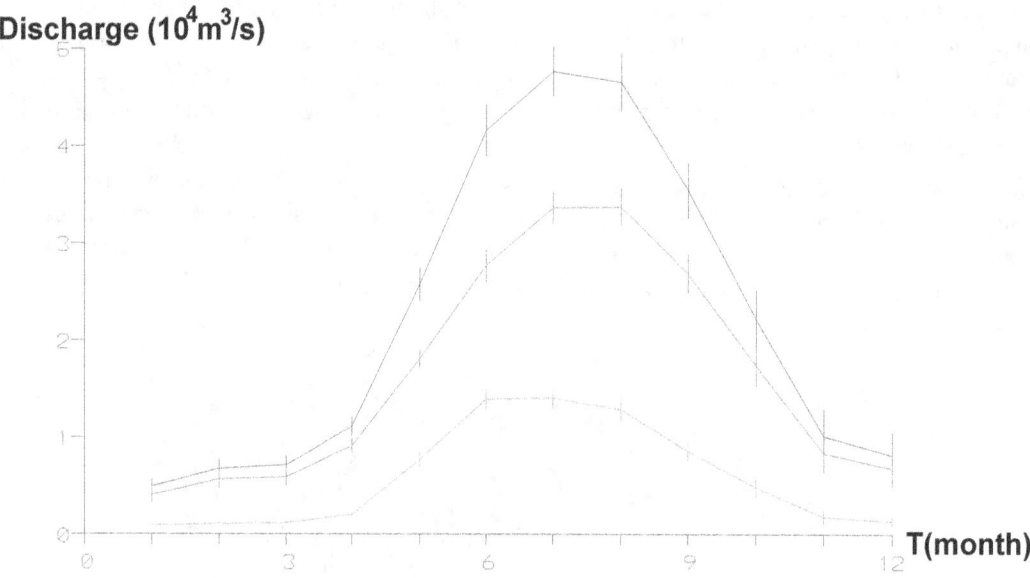

Discharge (10⁴m³/s)

T(month)

Figure 2. **Model simulated monthly climatology (seasonal cycle) of freshwater discharge derived from the 41-year simulations (1958–1998) and standard deviations (vertical bars). Black line is the total discharge into the Gulf of Alaska; the blue line is the line source and the red is the point source.**

Hydrological Modeling in the Lena River Basin

Xieyao Maa, Tetsuzo Yasunaria, Tetsuo Ohatac, and Yoshihiro Fukushimae

The Lena River is one of the four largest rivers flowing into the Arctic Ocean. The river freezes over completely from early December to late April and the flood dominated by snowmelt occurs with the river break-up in May–June. In order to determine the mechanism of the runoff formation, a hydrological modeling investigation was carried out in the period of 1986–2000. The model is composed of four submodels: one-dimensional soil-vegetation-atmosphere transfer (SVAT) model, runoff formation model, river routing model, and river ice model, developed by Ma and Fukushima (2002). The domain of the study area was established between 52°–72° N and 100°–140° E. Forty meteorological gages' data over the domain come from GAME-Siberia Committee. Three hydrological gages were selected to check the model performance. The results show that 1) the timing of flood rising and flood peak could be modeled for the selected hydrological stations, which present the entire basin (Kusur), the upper and midstream portions of the Lean (Tabaga), and a main tributary of the Lena (Verkhoyanskiy Perevoz); 2) river-freeze processes delay the spring, snowmelt-dominated flood by about 23 days at Tabaga; 3) estimates of annual runoff were sufficiently accurate (within 20 mm on average and 8.85%) at Kusur; 4) the total flood volume during May–July at Kusur is contributed by snowmelt.

Changes in Lena River Streamflow Hydrology: Human Impacts vs. Natural Variations

Daqing Yang and Douglas Kane

This study systematically analyzes long-term (1936–1999) monthly discharge records for the major sub-basins within the Lena River watershed in order to document significant streamflow hydrology changes induced by human activities (particularly reservoirs) and by natural variations/changes. The results show that the upper streams of the watershed, without much human impact, experience a runoff increase in winter, spring, and (particularly) summer seasons, and a discharge decrease in the fall season. These changes in seasonal streamflow characteristics indicate a hydrologic regime shift toward early snowmelt and higher summer streamflow, perhaps due to regional climate warming and permafrost degradation in the southern parts of Siberia. The results also demonstrate that reservoir regulations have significantly altered the monthly discharge regime in the lower parts of the Lena river basin. Because of a large dam in west Lena River, summer (high) flows at the outlet of the Vilui valley have been reduced by up to 55% and winter (low) flows have been increased by up to 30 times. These alterations, plus streamflow changes in the upper Lena regions, lead to strong upward trends (up to 90%) in monthly discharge at the basin outlet during the low flow months and weak increases (5–10%) in the high flow season. Monthly flow records at the basin outlet have been reconstructed by a regression method to reduce reservoir impacts. Trend analyses and comparisons between the observed and reconstructed monthly flows show that, because of reservoir regulations, discharge records observed at the Lena basin outlet do not always represent natural changes and variations. They tend to underestimate the natural runoff trends in summer and overestimate the trends in both winter and fall seasons. Therefore, cold season discharge increase identified at the mouth of the Lena basin is not all caused naturally, but is the combined effect of reservoir regulation and natural runoff changes in the unregulated upper sub-basins. This study clearly illustrates the importance of human activities in regional and global environment changes, and points to a need to examine human impacts in other large high-latitude watersheds.

Streamflow Response to Seasonal Snowcover Extent Changes in Large Siberian Watersheds

Daqing Yang, David Robinson, Yuanyuan Zhao, and Thomas Estilow

This study uses remotely sensed long-term (1966–1999) weekly snowcover extent data to investigate snowmelt runoff response to seasonal snowcover change in the large Siberian watersheds (the Ob, Yenisei, and Lena basins). It quantified the seasonal cycles and variations of snowcover extent and river streamflow, and identified a clear correspondence of river streamflow to seasonal snowcover extent change, i.e. an association of low streamflow with high snowcover extent during the

cold season, and an increase in discharge associated with a decrease of snowcover extent during the melt periods. This study also examined and compared the weekly mean streamflow with the weekly basin snowcover extent for the study period.

The results revealed a very strong linkage between the streamflow and snowcover extent change during the spring melt season over the large Siberian watersheds, and developed a statistically significant weekly runoff-snowcover relation. This relation suggests a practical procedure of using remotely sensed snowcover information for snowmelt runoff forecasting over the large northern watersheds. Analyses of extreme (high/low) streamflow cases (years) and the associated snowcover conditions indicate an association of high (low) flood peak with late (early) snowmelt in the Ob and Yenisei basins. Comparisons of snowmelt timing with peak flow show different associations between these two variables among the large Siberian rivers. These results demonstrate that the NOAA weekly snowcover extent data are useful for understanding and predicting streamflow changes in the arctic regions. Snowcover water equivalent data/products obtained by remote sensing technology and in-situ snow observations are currently being examined for what we expect will eventually improve hydrologic forecasts over the large northern watersheds.

Hydrological Modeling of Imnavait Creek, Alaska's North Slope

Imke Schramm

A new process-based, spatially distributed Hydrological Model (TopoFlow) is used to quantitatively simulate the water and energy fluxes in an Alaskan watershed. Imnavait Creek is a small watershed (1.5 km^2) located in the northern foothills of the Brooks Range ($68^0 30'$ N, $149^0 15'$ W) and drains into the Kuparuk River. Two peculiar characteristics: (i) Imnavait creek is a beaded stream and (ii) water tracks are efficient at conveying water down the slope during snowmelt and rainstorms.

Continuous permafrost underlies the active layer which, by the end of the summer season, reaches depths between 40 to 60 cm. Tussock tundra is the typical vegetation. The organic layer varies from about 50 cm in the valley bottom to around 10 cm on the slopes and ridges. The model is run using a collection of field data: Hourly climate and soil data (precipitation, long wave and short wave radiation, and profiles of air and soil temperature). Other field data collection includes discharge measurements (flume), snow survey for the calculation of snow water equivalent (SWE), soil physical properties, and channel characteristics.

The model simulates various physical processes including snow ablation, subsurface, overland and channel flow, soil thawing, and evapotranspiration. Predictions are made for the discharge at the outlet and will later include spatially-distributed soil moisture.

Results using TopoFlow are presented and compared to measured discharge and SWE. First results indicate that the onset of snowmelt does not correspond well with the measured data because the model does not include the snow damming effect. Simulated hydrographs for the summer runoff period 2001 with different settings demonstrate that the different components of the water circle are represented in the model.

Theme 3: Sea Ice, Oceanography, and Geochemistry

Dispersal of River Discharge in the Siberian Arctic and its Impact on the Sea-ice Environment: Lessons to be Learned for the North Slope Region?

Hajo Eicken and Igor Dmitrenko

The interactions between river water discharged onto Arctic shelves and the sea-ice cover are manifold and complex. Following river break-up, part of the spring floodwaters typically flood the surface of landfast ice, accelerating ice decay and scouring under-ice sediments as a result of localized, high-energy drainage flow. These processes have been studied for some time in various parts of the Arctic and are fairly easy to detect and monitor with available remote sensing tools. Another type of interaction occurs during the freeze-up and winter periods, when river water that has not been fully dispersed and mixed into the offshore shelf waters can have significant impacts on ice formation and growth. These processes are more difficult to observe

because they are confined to the bottom of the ice cover and the waters underneath (and occur during a period where extreme weather and darkness hamper some remote-sensing approaches).

During the past decade, a detailed, large-scale Russian-German collaborative program (with some U.S. involvement) has examined hydrologic, oceanographic and geologic processes over the Laptev Sea shelf in central northern Siberia (e.g., Kassens et al., 1998). As the Laptev Sea shelf receives on the order of 500 km^3 of freshwater from the Lena River annually, it might serve as a model system, with the large amounts of data compiled for this region helping guide and validate freshwater discharge modeling and field-observation efforts.

Here, we report on recent studies of the impact of river discharge on the Laptev sea-ice environment (Eicken et al., submitted). A combination of remote sensing techniques (in particular synthetic aperture radar, SAR), field observations and analysis of sea-ice core data yielded the following findings: (1) The dielectric properties of low-salinity sea ice allow for mapping of brackish ice/water distribution as well as the detection of bottomfast sea ice in estuarine areas; (2) building on previous work by Macdonald et al. (1999) it was possible to obtain time series of under-ice water salinities through the water stable-isotope analysis of ice cores, allowing for derivation of under-ice water spreading rates (among the highest reported in the Arctic so far on this scale); (3) combining remote-sensing and ice-core data, it was shown that of the Laptev landfast ice (ca. 160,000 km^2) roughly two thirds are composed of river water, locking up about one quarter of the annual Lena discharge and contributing to a mean inner shelf residence time of river water of more than a year.

While the magnitude of freshwater discharge from Alaska North Slope rivers is significantly smaller than that of the Lena, discharge dispersal modeling efforts need to address the question as to whether similar processes need to be taken into account in the coastal Beaufort and Chukchi seas. Here, remote sensing and ice-core analysis may help in quantitative assessments of the role of river-water/sea-ice interaction.

References

Eicken, H., Dmitrenko, I., Tyshko, K., Darovskikh, A., Dierking, W., Blahak, U., Groves, J., and Kassens, H. (submitted) Zonation of the Laptev Sea landfast ice cover and its importance in a frozen estuary. Submitted to Global Planet. Change.

Kassens, H., Dmitrenko, I., Rachold, V., Thiede, J., and Timokhov, L. (1998) Russian and German Scientists explore the Arctic's Laptev Sea and its climate system. Eos, Transact. Am. Geophys. Union 79(27):317–323.

Macdonald, R.W., Carmack, E.C., Paton, D.W. (1999) Using the $\delta 18^o$ composition in landfast ice as a record of arctic estuarine processes. Mar. Chem. 65:3–24.

Arctic Shelf Fronts and their Relation to Freshwater Discharge

Igor Belkin, Nikolay Doronin, and Mikhail Kulakov

We will present a comparative analysis of the Arctic shelf fronts whose origins are largely related to freshwater discharge of northern rivers. Geographically, this survey is circumpolar and includes the following shelf seas and major rivers that empty into them:

- Beaufort Sea (Mackenzie, Colville)
- White Sea (Onega, Severnaya Dvina)
- Barents Sea (Mezen', Pechora)
- Kara Sea (Ob', Taz, Yenisei, Pyasina)
- Laptev Sea (Khatanga, Lena, Yana)
- East-Siberian Sea (Indigirka, Kolyma)
- Bering Sea (Yukon, Kuskokwim)

We will present in situ and remote sensing data on the Arctic shelf fronts and their seasonal and interannual variability. Among the most valuable data sets, the newly acquired Russian CTD data from the Siberian seas (see Table) stands out since this data has not been previously analyzed to detect shelf fronts. To study these fronts from satellite data we used the Pathfinder AVHRR SST 9 km resolution twice-daily data from January 1985 through December 1996 that has been processed, mapped, and analyzed at the University of Rhode Island.

Seasonal and interannual variability of shelf fronts is related to respective variations in river discharge of adjacent rivers. Some rivers could control frontal characteristics far downstream from their estuaries, e.g. Yukon discharge is advected into the Chukchi Sea where it affects the Kotzebue Sound front and Barrow Canyon front, and influences shelf fronts of the Beaufort Sea. Similarly, the great Siberian rivers such as Ob', Yenisei, and Lena affect shelf fronts located hundreds of miles away. Since the fronts' location and structure exert significant control over shelf sedimentation regime and cross-frontal exchange of nutrients, this study contributes to a wide range of applications, from marine geology and offshore technology to biological oceanography and fisheries, through improvement of numerical models of the coastal Arctic Ocean.

Table 1. Newly acquired Russian CTD data set from the Siberian seas.

Year	Date	Number of CTD stations	Area of survey	
			Latitude	*Longitude*
Kara Sea				
1993	16.09 - 13.10	145	70° 00' - 78° 40'	56° 00' – 104° 00'
1994	23.08 – 24.09	142	68° 00' – 78° 30'	57° 50' – 88° 10'
1994	17.06 – 28.06	6	70° 10' – 77° 40'	66° 20' – 103° 45'
	14.08 – 23.08	4		
1995	17.8 – 7.09	108	68° 20' – 80° 00'	59° 40' – 86° 00'
1995	10.08 – 14.08	6	69° 45' – 77° 45'	60° 30' – 105° 40'
	8.09 – 18.09	20		
1997	13.09 – 25.09	59	72° 00' - 74° 00'	72° 40' – 82° 50'
1999	24.08 – 8.09	37	72° 00' – 74° 30'	74° 00' – 80° 00'
2000	19.08 – 24.08	15	57° 40' – 84° 30'	70° 40' – 74° 50'
2000	4.09 – 19.09	24	70° 00' – 77° 00'	74° 10' – 85° 45'
2001	14.08 – 11.09	83	69° 00' – 78° 00'	72° 15' – 89° 20'
Laptev Sea				
1993	10.08 – 13.09	131	71° 40' – 77° 10'	114° 00' –140° 40'
1994	3.09 – 26.09	102	71° 45' – 76° 30'	114° 15' – 136° 45'
1994	29.06 – 8.07	4	74° 20' – 76° 40'	113° 25' – 138° 00'
	31.07 – 11.08	2		
1995	6.10 – 23.10	65	71° 05' – 80° 10'	102° 30' – 139° 15'
1995	14.08 – 20.08	9	71° 05' – 77° 45'	96° 45' – 141° 30'
	30.08 – 9.09	25		
1998	1.09 – 18.09	55	73° 30' – 77° 50'	115° 50' – 133° 50'
1999	27.08 – 8.09	30	71° 30' – 76° 55'	114° 35' – 135° 40'
2000	3.09 – 15.09	48	71° 45' – 77° 15'	123° 45' – 135° 30'
East-Siberian Sea				
1994	10.07 – 29.07	6	70° 15' – 75° 40'	147° 10' – 170° 25'
1995	20.08 – 30.08	30	69° 40' – 76° 10'	141° 15' – 170° 30'
1995	24.08 – 29.08	45	69° 30' – 71° 20'	164° 00' – 180° 00'
2003	10.09 – 20.09	44	70° 00' – 74° 50'	140° 20' – 178° 30'
Chukchi Sea				
1990	3.09 – 23.09	122	65° 45' – 74° 10'	178° 00'E – 159° 40'W
1990	4.10 – 20.10	141	65° 40' – 74° 00'	178° 00'E –159° 25'W
1992	21.09 – 4.10	108	65° 00' – 71° 10'	177° 25'W –158° 50'W
1993	21.09 – 10.10	120	64° 00' – 74° 20'	177° 50' E –154° 45'W
1994	22.09 – 10.10	60	65° 45' – 71° 45'	175° 00'W –159° 30'W
1995	28.08 – 30.08	31	66° 40' – 70° 00'	179° 10'E-169° 00'W
1995	10.09 – 30.09	208	64° 35' – 73° 00'	177° 40'E –157° 20'W

The Flow of Alaskan Coastal Current from the Gulf of Alaska to the Beaufort Sea–Challenges and Opportunities

Wieslaw Maslowski and Jaclyn Clement

The flow of relatively fresh water along the Alaskan coast from the North Pacific, through the Bering Sea, into the Arctic Ocean is typically defined as the Alaska Coastal Current (ACC). The southern portion of this current, from the Gulf of Alaska to the Aleutian Islands, has been most studied (Schumacher and Reed 1986; Stabeno et al., 1995; Royer, 1998, Ladd et al., 2004). However, understanding of the important role it plays in the life history of juvenile salmon or Steller sea lions and in the transport and fate of spilled oil in the Gulf of Alaska requires further research. For example, improved knowledge of transient circulation features (e.g. eddies and meanders) may provide important insights into their effects on seasonal and interannual transport of nutrients, zooplankton, larvae, and fish across the front formed by the ACC.

Much less is known of the pathways and water properties of the ACC downstream of the Aleutian Islands, in the Bering, Chukchi, and Beaufort seas. Complex physical mechanisms involved in mixing and advection in the southeastern Bering Sea, tides, river runoff, and seasonal sea ice cover over the shelves, and strong atmospheric forcing during fall/winter storms make this region quite challenging for field and modeling investigations. Understanding of these complex and variable interactions and feedbacks is critical to explaining the flow of ACC further north, in the Chukchi and Beaufort seas. The preconditioning of Pacific water passing Bering Strait and contributions from freshwater inputs and salt from coastal polynyas determine the dynamics and properties of the coastal flow along the northern Alaska coasts.

In this talk, we will outline the main physical and numerical challenges in modeling the ACC as a continuous flow from the Gulf of Alaska to the Beaufort Sea and will discuss opportunities to address some of them. Results from a regional ice-ocean model will be presented to illustrate potential capabilities for realistic modeling of the ACC at time scales from days to decades.

Riverine Transport and Dispersion of Freshwater, Suspended Sediment, Organic Carbon, and Trace Metals in the Coastal Beaufort Sea During the Spring Floods

Robert Rember, J.H. Trefry, and R.P. Trocine

Concentrations of suspended sediment, organic carbon, and dissolved metals in water from the Sagavanirktok and Kuparuk rivers were determined during the spring floods of 2001, 2002, and 2004. All three of these components of river water increased in concentration during peak flow in response to the flushing of soils and surface ponds during the spring floods. Then, this large pulse of river water was tracked and detected under a 2 m thick lens of ice at distances of 10–20 km offshore in the coastal Beaufort Sea. Concentrations of dissolved metals below the turbid riverine discharge were very low and typical of levels found during the open water period in summer and fall. However, concentrations of suspended sediment in the deeper water under the ice were very low. During a three week study in May 2004, a more detailed study of offshore transport of river water under the ice was conducted by sampling through ~30 holes drilled offshore from the mouths of the Sagavanirktok and Kuparuk rivers. Sampling was designed to give both a temporal and spatial perspective to freshwater discharge under the ice. A CTD and current meter were deployed through the ice and multiple samples were collected from each hole for DOC, P, N, $\delta18^{O}$ and a suite of dissolved trace metals.

Distribution of Freshwater Sources in the Western Arctic Ocean Derived from Chemical Tracers Oxygen Isotope Ratio, and Alkalinity

Michiyo Yamamoto-Kawai, Noriyuki Tanaka, Sergey Pivovarov, and Leonid Timokhov

Freshwater distribution in the Arctic Ocean has a key role in the regional and also the global climate through affecting the heat transport by changing surface stratification in the Arctic Ocean and also the deep convection in the Greenland Sea. River runoff provides the largest freshwater amount to the Arctic Ocean. Precipitation–evaporation over the ocean and the Pacific water coming through the Bering Strait also provide additional freshwater. Furthermore, formation and melting of sea-ice can alter the distribution of freshwater. The western Arctic is the region where both massive freshwater input and active sea ice melting/formation occur. Two chemical tracers, oxygen isotope ratio ($\delta 18^O$) and total alkalinity (TA) are used to distinguish freshwater sources and to investigate their distributions in the western Arctic Ocean.

From horizontal distribution of freshwater sources and relationships between salinity, $\delta 18^O$, and TA, the flow pattern of river water can be pictured as follows: Russian river water flows out of the shelf between the Mendeleyev Ridge and the Lomonosov Ridge, enters into the deeper part of the Ocean, and flows toward the western part of Fram Strait. Part of this freshwater enters into the Canadian basin to the east, where high fraction of river water is found but the fraction of Mackenzie River water is small. This may suggest that Mackenzie River water should exit from the basin relatively fast, probably through the Canadian Archipelago.

Accumulation of freshwater in the Canadian Basin is maintained by advection of water from the adjacent shallow shelves. The dense shelf water formed during winter enters into the layer between surface and Atlantic origin water and can be identified by the nutrient maximum. Although the high concentration of nutrients of the water points to the winter Pacific water as a major source, our analysis indicates significant contributions of other shelf waters. Three types of shelf-derived water are suggested to form the nutrient maximum layer in the Canadian Basin. 1) Winter Pacific water with rejected brine during sea ice formation. 2) shelf water formed on the Beaufort shelf. 3) shelf water formed on the Chukchi/East Siberian seas, from fresher shelf water containing summer Pacific water and/or Russian river water. The third type of shelf water seems to contribute more than the second type of water. These shelf waters vertically transport freshwater from the surface to the deeper layer and accumulate in the Canadian basin.

We appreciate Drs. Murata and Shimada of JAMSTEC for providing unpublished data from the past Arctic expeditions by R/V Mirai.

Intraseasonal and Interdecadal Variability of Arctic Freshwater and Heat Budget

Jia Wang and Inna Shapiro

Using four decades (1950–1989) of hydrographic and sea-ice cover data in the Arctic Ocean and subpolar seas, we systematically examine the climatological mean, interdecadal, and interseasonal variability of freshwater storage in both liquid and solid (ice) forms. We found that the mean liquid freshwater storage is 201,400 (168,975) km^3 for summer and (winter), which is about 2–2.5 times the historical estimate (Arctic Ocean only) of 80,000 km^3 (Aagaard and Carmack 1989). The solid freshwater stored in the sea ice is estimated to be 23,228 (34,842) km^3 for 2 m (3 m) mean ice thickness, which is consistent with a previous estimate of 17,300 km^3.

The intraseasonal variation indicates that the summer-winter freshwater storage difference is about 32,645 km^3. Inter-decadal variability in FS has a positive correlation with the 10-year averaged Arctic Oscillation index and first SAT mode, while negative correlation with the sea-ice covers anomalies. Thus, the AO-related inter-decadal variability (or trend) is significant. The intra-seasonal variation of solid freshwater storage is 13,359 km^3, the difference between the winter storage of 28,902 km^3 and the summer storage of 15,543 km^3 (if the mean ice thickness is assumed 2 m). The Arctic Ocean is divided into five sub-regions. Freshwater storages in both liquid and solid forms are estimated for the four decades.

Appendix 3. Themes for Workshop.

Themes 1–3 Discussion (original notes)

Climate and Atmospheric Components
Introduced by David Atkinson
(Notes Jessie Cherry)

Jia: In global model hydrological scale is 200–400 m, can climate models resolve?

Laura: Not in her large-scale model.

General question: How sensitive are models to timing and location of freshwater inputs and total quantity in OGCMs (ocean general circulation models) i.e. on NAO/AO scales?

Wieslaw: 1980s–1990s cyclonic shift (Canadian basin) changed the residence time of river runoff in the arctic…more sensitivity studies necessary…

David: Sea ice forced by atmospheric circulation and thermal forces, which is the stronger forcing? What is responsible for disappearing sea ice?

Jia: Positive AO anomalous cyclonic circulation helps diverge sea ice out of the arctic into the GIN (Greenland, Island, and Norwegian) seas, negative AO anomalously anticyclonic circulation dominates, ice gets trapped in the Canada basin.

Seasonal cycle, winter Beaufort high, freshwater and sea ice trapped, summer, freshwater is relaxed and spreads out.

Wieslaw: Recent AO is more neutral, yet most melting in recent years. That suggests that thermal coupling may be really important.

What about the residence time of ice?

Jia: In hydrological modeling, how sensitive is energy balance on snow albedo?

Laura: quite sensitive, changes in timing of melt onset

Introduction by Laura Bowling
Talks in 3 areas:
Hydrology

USGS

Remote sensing techniques

Two tiers of model talks:

Small scale-topo model

Large scale-WATCLASS, Jia's model

Wieslaw: How far away are we from 50 year run-offs of rivers w/temps?

Laura: What resolutions do you want information? Temp is not done, that will take a while. Course resolution 100 km grid is almost ready.

Wieslaw: Ocean community needs location, daily temp, quant of runoff. 40–50 years. Line source is okay.

Bob Carlson: What is needed to understand coastal runoff. NWS uses one approach, is Prentki's [MMS's] need a long range planning tool, 20–30 years, versus, short term for use w/spills?

Dick: Yes, we need both, now. Use last year's data for hindcast, that's NOAA's approach.

Bob Carlson: 100 km x 100 km not very useful. Stakeholders want to know specific places, oceanographers have other needs.

Caryn: Need physical processes, goal is 1–3 km.

Dick: Some stakeholders need smaller scales

Bob Carlson: Oceanographers uncomfortable with coastal zone, so are hydrologists, we skip over that.

Dick: Landfast ice is a tricky area.

Wieslaw: Need more than one vertical grid cell, that's not good enough for shallow 60 m area

Jia: What are differences between Japanese, Canadian models, Vic?

Frank: Treat different parts of the cycle differently, we have emphasis in Canada.

Laura: PILPS 2e analyzed this. CLASS has peat. She's focused on lakes and wetlands and blowing snow (in VIC). Outliers in model intercomparisons are very useful to know what some models are doing right/wrong. Permafrost has not been tested well enough in the model.

Frank: Do we have enough data to verify/input to see if Permafrost schemes are good/bad?

Laura: The lack of good permafrost dynamics will make the freshwater runoff dataset have big error bars.

Stephan: Getting the hydrograph right is a good place to start.

Dick: That would be a good recommendation.

Jia: Can Larry's model be extrapolated to regional/ global scale?

Larry: No, we are process-oriented. Working w/ Lettenmier to see if we can nest our model in Vic. For example, testing vegetation changes helpful.

Bjerklie: Spring breakup key for heat transfer, nutrients. Models are focused on tundra regions, but what about mountains? 80% of Sag catchment is in the Brooks Range. Is it the same for other rivers? Is there a model that could handle the timing issues?

Larry: No, no work in the mountains, including measurements, we have no idea what is going on there.

Laura: another problem. No glaciers in the models!

Bjerklie: Lena? I don't know about physiography of Russian rivers.

Laura: Headwaters in Siberia are as far South as 45, steppes and high plateaus.

Igor: Reservoir on the rivers in Siberia? Effect of dams? Water mass transfer?

Dick: Reservoirs change heat regime, too.

Wieslaw: Hajo runoff onto land-fast ice, what is the residence time of river discharge onto land-fast ice?

Hajo: Ice decouples atmosphere dynamics from water, which is really forming a lake (like in Mack, Carmack's work) during winter.

Wieslaw: Residence time of Lena River water in coastal area? How is it affected by land fast ice?

Hajo: Need tracers to be able to separate other river (Yenesei). Prevents cross-shelf transport, becomes along-coast transport.

Larry: Frazzle ice layer that Robert mentioned. Has that been documented before? How wide-spread? Does it help maintain stratification?

It's in Hajo's book: Hajo: yes, it's been reported by Russians on the Russian shelves and others. We don't know how widespread.

Dick: Landfast ice off Prudue, no momentum transfer between atmosphere and ocean, once ice is there, runoff is going to stabilize that layer. Summer storms are what mixes it up.

Jia: OGMS, do they input Freshwater velocity? Could they do this?

Wieslaw: Need the data! Resolution of grid cell 50 km^2 ... how important is getting the runoff velocity right? He thinks there are more important problems.

Ron: Have you incorporated land fast ice?

Wieslaw: really difficult to get the anchor points, need to have the bathymetry features in the model, not resolved in the model. Need at least a climatology. This can probably be done once data is available. Flato's way to deal w/problem is to use isobaths (10 m), say the ice isn't moving. Most models have minimum shallow depth of 50 m, but mine is 10 m.

Theme 2 Discussion (original records)

How do you know where there is continuous or discontinuous permafrost?

Model vs. observation: combine both to estimate discharge; modeling + remote sensing.

Goal of models is to understand processes, but also good to distribute discharge.

Larry: Necessary to re-establish stream gages. And precipitation of course.

Dick: Important that experts say that more stations are needed.

Stefan: Snow course measurements important as well. Two classes of models: fine and course resolution. For large scale models resolution is coarser than measurements to compare to. E.g. every grid cell generates a runoff. If grid cells are bigger than streamflow measurements, there is no possibility to validate the model.

Laura: Large scale models cannot go into more detail. The problem is that there is no medium scale model, so there is a kind of grey zone in between both. The computation speed is a problem because most models run on PCs and cannot be run on supercomputers.

Frank: Concerning the validation of models: we should focus on a few basins to have a kind of research area with very detailed data. But if the model works for one watershed there is no way to conclude that it works in another area with e.g. another topography.

Larry: Excess to watersheds in mountain area is a problem. There are no roads and almost no glacier measurements. Is there so much water coming out of the glaciers in North Slope that it is important for hydrological modeling and climate change research?

Answer?

Frank: Data verification: There was one big data collection for three years (BOREAS) which are used for all kinds of model verification. That could be an idea for funding, to start one big data collection for a certain area and limited time.

Channel slopes: high resolution DEMs are not available for the whole North Slope area. But all models are based on DEMs, so that could be important.

Freeze up and break up of lakes in models? It is not represented in any model. There is no physical reason why one could not model it, but river ice is not included so far.

Radar data are used so far to monitor river break up.

Depletion snow cover: satellite images could be useful to monitor snow cover.

Laura: Remote sensing for soil moisture, river break up, snow cover, active layer depth.

Larry: Soil moisture is very important. Continuous data at various data is needed.

??: we can get soil wetness, but soil moisture is almost impossible. From SAR you can get … best ones are???

Larry: Profiles of radiation are necessary.

Laura: δ apor flux over the whole winter would be great, but very difficult to collect and to maintain stations. There is no possibility so far to validate sublimation and snow distribu-tion from model.

Larry: 10% of summer precipitation came as con-densation at Betty Pingo site, so it is impor-tant to measure.

??: There are some data series for that in the North Slope.

Frank: it would be good to have an internet side or something to have an overview which data are available, at least for the North Slope. Ev-eryone could put his data there or links where to find them.

Dick: We try to do that, but …

Frank: SWE and snow depth, soil moisture, and soil temperature at the same time.

Stefan: remote sensing does not give you any use-ful data without having ground measurements (concerning snow course). That would help to avoid errors from snow gages.

Frank: Runoff components measurements to differ-entiate between base flow, active layer flow…

Laura: Concerning lakes: There is a very complex drainage network especially during snow melt. And in the coastal region.

The storage component is important (in lakes…). How do you model lake depth?

We used radar and model simulations combined to get lake depth.

Remote sensing of river ice: there is flow under the ice–how is this represented in models? Could winter flow be modeled?

There are winter flow measurements, but the quali-ty varies from station to station. It's a problem that expensive equipment could be damaged.

Comment on winter measurement: (Rich) Zero flow because instruments are not located where flow occurs.

Radar images where used to look at ice patches on rivers.

Frank: Water temperature is the first measurement that should be made in terms of chemistry.

2. Vorne links: we normally take temperature mea-surements when stream gaging.

Small temperature changes can be significant for chemistry, species changes–there are biologi-cal reasons to monitor water temperature.

Ratio of permafrost and non-permafrost region: more thermokarst results in more sediment transport. To model the carbon cycle, sediment transport is of importance.

Frank: Prediction of discharge in ungaged basins… If we did error bars on our predictions that would help, because to give out one specific number is not really true. We modelers should start doing that.

It is difficult to include the errors in the input data.

There are several kinds of errors: in measurements, the model processing and ? – different error boxes.

Laura: Questions and recommendations related to the other groups?

Frank: Downscaling of precipitation (physical reason?).

Averaging of model predictions to limit the single model errors.

Laura: Data needs.

Method recommendations?

Combining different methods of data collection: remote sensing, modeling, and ground measurements. Modeling is the only way to go back in time–and then a tool to go forward.

Recommendation not only to focus on large basin gaging. Small basin measurements also important. Seward Peninsula and Kotzebue would be representative to calibrate the models for the north slope. Eastern Alaska is not covered yet.

Larry: We don't know a lot about aufeis fields.

Laura: (Dis-) continuous permafrost represented in models?

Frank: Planned for the future to better represent.

Larry: Kind of representation in small-scale model (?)

Laura: Integrated Studies? Dealing with the grey zone?

Vorne links: How does road dust effect?

Larry: Impact of road network on wildlife and ?

USGS stations

High quality DEM

Validation Needs

Permafrost

Question: Discontinuous permafrost–how do you know where to put it in model, changes through time? Workshop on permafrost modeling in two weeks here.

Runoff fields could use mix of hydrographic stations and models.

Reestablish gages at long term sites.

Ideas-measure

Snow courses

Water temperatures

Precipitation

Large scale models could get to 1–2 km in theory with understanding of hydrology. Finer resolution is possible by computer.

Verification

Need more stations toward mountains.

Road dust and hydrology. Bird use in spring.

Increasing glacier melt could relate to increasing Sag River flow through recent decades.

Suggestion for concentrated study on a few/couple watersheds: Active layer measurements, snow cover and depth, soil moisture profile and temperature, total radiation balance, eddy covariance, runoff component rates/quantities, lake stage, lake area (storage in lakes, ponds, channels, soils). Lidar data being collected in NPRA, but not clear how these data being used. Mackenzie Delta Lidar, also. Expand Lidar or other to get consistent DEM across North Slope. Need fine resolution.

AK North Slope, only Sag flows all winter. Canning has springs, could have flow?

USGS does measure temperature in discharge, but data hard to find.

Temperature changes could be biologically important; do not know what delta temperature becomes important oceanography.

Uranium series signature appears to be different in permafrost vs. discontinuous permafrost areas. Perhaps a method to track changes in permafrost with global change?

Need to develop statistical error on hydrology data.

Seward Peninsula as a proxy North Slope—regage rivers. Redo in Canning and ANWR.

Aufeis fields in some areas.

Combine modeling with better gaging and remote sensing, some local.

Models don't get breakup and freeze up dates right.

Remote sensing of snow cover.

Need web link for North Slope data—or make sure can find existing one(s).

Develop methods to downscale large scale gridded data to hydrology scales.

Goal of real time model on web.

Discussion of themes (missed part)

Albedo set in Laura Bowling model

> Melting and accumulation time curves for albedo of snow.

Theme 2 Moderator:

Areas of hydro observations, remote sensing techniques, two tiers of modeling talks (small scale and large scale).

Q. How far from 50-year hydrology run with temperature, time, and volume to ocean.

R. Depends on resolution needed. Temperature not usually provided.

Ocean community–at least daily on 10 km grid for 50 years. Based on latlong–line source for ungaged OK.

Question–scale for MMS needs 20–30 year forecast, but hindcast needs basin to get there, want 1–3 km scale. Need basin to get physics right.

Different hydrology models depend on other prime issues,

For North Slope need permafrost. Moderator–best model not evaluated yet.

Comment: need agreement on what needed to test and needed to validate and compare. Mechanistic, but not tested against.

Q. How best to convert small models to large scale–Not best approach. The small models are process models–not same purpose. Perhaps nested models best. (ex. Tussock to brush tundra).

Q. Breakup–short with timing–heat and nutrients. But what's happening in Brooks Range? Timing is different for different rivers. No data in mountains.

Q. What are Siberian Rivers like? Not Arctic, extend far south, have managed flow.

Theme 3:

Capture of Lena freshwater in local sea ice–but ice melts. Yes, but long extent of landfast ice decouples with coastal circulation. Does a couple of months longer extent of freshwater nearby matter? It does spot cross shelf transport, keeps freshwater on the shelf.

How stable is freshwater layer from rivers? No momentum transport from wind under landfast ice. Rivers breakup, May–June, Ocean July–layer stays until storms breakup in summer.

How to put fast ice in models? Problem with anchor points, not really good. Landfast ice zone is a problem.

Appendix 4. SIOM Workshop Participants

Johnny L. Aiken
Acting Land Management Regulations Manager
North Slope Borough Planning Dept
1920 Takpuk St., P.O. Box 69
Barrow, Alaska 99723
Phone: 907-852-0440
E-mail: Johnny.Aiken@north-slope.org

David E. Atkinson
Assistant Professor
IARC/Atmospheric Sciences
University of Alaska Fairbanks
930 Koyukuk Dr. / Box 757335
Fairbanks, Alaska 99775-7335
Phone: 907-474-1126
E-mail: datkinson@iarc.uaf.edu

Igor M. Belkin
Graduate School of Oceanography
University of Rhode Island
215 South Ferry Road
Narragansett, Rhode Island 02882
Phone: 401-874-6533
E-mail: ibelkin@gso.uri.edu

Svetlana Berezovskaya
Water & Environmental Research Center
University of Alaska Fairbanks
305 Tanana Dr., 485 Duckering Bldg
Fairbanks, Alaska 99775
Phone: 907-474-2783
E-mail: ffslb2@uaf.edu

Heather R. Best
Hydrologic Technician
U.S.G.S. Fairbanks Field Headquarters
3400 Shell Street
Fairbanks, Alaska 99701
Phone: 907-479-5645
E-Mail: hbest@usgs.gov

David M. Bjerklie
Hydrologist
U.S.G.S.
101 Pitkin Street
East Hartford, Connecticut 06108
Phone: 860-291-6770
E-mail: dmbjerkl@usgs.gov

William R. Bolton
Graduate Assistant
Water & Environmental Research Center
462 Duckering
University of Alaska Fairbanks
Fairbanks, Alaska 99775
Phone: 907-474-7975
E-mail: ffwrb@uaf.edu

Laura C. Bowling
Assistant Professor
Department of Agronomy
Purdue University
Lilly Hall of Life Sciences
915 W. State Street
West Lafayette, Indiana 47907-2054
Phone: 765-494-8051
E-mail: bowling@purdue.edu

Robert F. Carlson
Doctor/Professor
Dept. of Civil & Environmental Engineering
University of Alaska Fairbanks
237 Duckering Bldg., P.O. Box 755900
Fairbanks, Alaska 99775-5900
Phone: 907-474-6120
E-mail: ffrfc1@uaf.edu

Jessica E. Cherry
Graduate Research Assistant
Columbia University
Lamont-Doherty Earth Observatory
61 Route 9W, Ocean 206
Palisades, New York 10964
Phone: 845-365-8327
E-Mail: jcherry@ldeo.columbia.edu

Claude Duguay
Professor
Geophysical Institute
University of Alaska Fairbanks
903 Koyukuk Drive
Fairbanks, Alaska 99775
Phone: 907-474-6832
E-mail: claude.duguay@gi.alaska.edu

Hajo Eicken
Associate Professor
Geophysical Institute
University of Alaska Fairbanks
903 Koyukuk Dr./P.O. Box 757320
Fairbanks, AK 99775-7320
Phone: 907-474-7280
E-mail: hajo.eicken@gi.alaska.edu

Steven A. Frenzel
Chief
Water Resources Office
USGS Alaska Science Center
U.S. Geological Survey
4230 University Dr., Suite 201
Anchorage, Alaska 99508
Phone: 907-786-7107
E-mail: sfrenzel@usgs.gov

Meibing Jin
Research Assistant Professor
International Arctic Research Center
University of Alaska Fairbanks
P.O..Box 757335 / 930 Koyukuk Dr.
Fairbanks, Alaska 99775-7335
Phone: 907-474-2442
E-mail: mbj@iarc.uaf.edu

Joe Klein
Hydrologist
ADF&G, SF/RTS
333 Raspberry Road
Anchorage, Alaska 99518
Phone: 907-267-2148
E-mail: joe_klein@fishgame.state.ak.us

Keith Echelmeyer
Professor of Geophysics
Geophysical Institute
University of Alaska Fairbanks
903 Koyukuk Drive
Fairbanks, Alaska 99775
Phone: 907-474-7477
E-mail: kechel@gi.alaska.edu

Susan Flora
HazMats Contaminants - NPRA
Bureau of Land Management
1150 University Avenue
Fairbanks, Alaska 99709
Phone: 907-474-2303
E-mail: sflora@blm.gov

Larry Hinzman
Water & Environmental Research Center
Institute of Northern Engineering
P.O. Box 755860
437 Duckering Building
University of Alaska Fairbanks
Fairbanks, Alaska 99775-5860
Phone: 907-474-7331
E-mail: ffdh@uaf.edu

Michiyo Kawaii
Post-Doc
International Arctic Research Center
University of Alaska Fairbanks
P.O. Box 757335 / 930 Koyukuk Drive
Fairbanks, Alaska 99775-7335
Phone: 907-474-1524
E-mail: yamami@iarc.uaf.edu

Richard Kemnitz
Hydrologist - NPRA
Bureau of Land Management
1150 University Avenue
Fairbanks, Alaska 99709
Phone: 907-474-2225
E-mail: rkemnitz@blm.gov

Rebecca Kyle
Hydro Tech / Student
USGS / FFO
3400 Shell Street
Fairbanks, Alaska 99701
Phone: 907-479-5645 x232
E-mail: rkyle@usgs.gov

Shusun Li
Research Professor
Geophysical Institute
University of Alaska Fairbanks
903 Koyukuk Drive
Fairbanks, Alaska 99775
Phone: 907-474-7676
E-mail: sli@asf.alaska.edu

Michael R. Lilly
President
Geo-Watersheds Scientific
650 Eton Boulevard
Fairbanks, Alaska 99709
Phone: 907-479-8891
E-mail: mlilly@gwscientific.com

Wieslaw Maslowski
Research Associate Professor
Naval Postgraduate School
Oceanography Department
833 Dyer Road
Monterey, California 93943
Phone: 831-656-3162
E-mail: maslowsk@nps.edu

David F. Meyer
Hydrologist, Data Section Chief
U.S. Geological Survey
Alaska Science Center
4230 University Dr., Suite 201
Anchorage, Alaska 99508
Phone: 907-786-7141
E-mail: dfmeyer@usgs.gov

Ronald J. Lai
Minerals Management Service/DOI
381 Elden Street
Herndon, Virginia 20170
Phone: 703-787-1714
E-Mail: ronald.lai@mms.gov

Anna Liljedahl
Institute of Northern Engineering
Water & Environmental Research Center
Room 447 Duckering Building
University of Alaska Fairbanks
Fairbanks, Alaska
Phone: 907-474-6243
E-mail: ftakl@uaf.edu or annald00@student.umu.se

Xieyao Ma
Frontier Research Center for Global Change
3173-25 Showamachi, Kanazawa-ku,
Yokohama 236-0001, Japan
Phone: 81-45-778-5546
E-mail: xyma@jamstec.go.jp

Larry Merculieff
Alaska Native Science Commission
Seven Generations Consulting
429 L Street
Anchorage, Alaska 99501
Phone: 907-258-2672
E-mail: lmerculieff@netscape.net

Edward Plumb
Hydrologist/Meteorologist
National Weather Service Forecast Office
930 Koyukuk Dr., Room 351
Fairbanks, Alaska 99708
Phone: 907-458-3714
E-mail: edward.plumb@noaa.gov

Stefan Pohl
National Water Research Institute
11 Innovation Blvd.
Saskatoon, Saskatchewan,
Canada S7N 3H5
Phone: 306-975-5752
E-mail: Stefan.Pohl@ec.gc.ca

Robert Rember
Research Technician
International Arctic Research Center
University of Alaska Fairbanks
P.O. Box 757335 / 930 Koyukuk Dr.
Fairbanks, Alaska 99775-7335
Phone: 907-474-2795
E-mail: rrember@iarc.uaf.edu

Frank Seglenieks
Research Engineering
University of Waterloo
200 University Avenue West
Waterloo, Ontario
Canada N2L 3G1
Phone: 519-88-4567 x6112
E-mail: frseglen@uwaterloo.ca

Kristin Susens
Graduate Research Assistant
Water & Environment Research Centr
P.O. Box 755860 / 435 Duckering
University of Alaska Fairbanks
Fairbanks, Alaska 99775-5860
Phone: 907-474-2713
E-mail: ftkms2@uaf.edu

John E. Walsh
President's Professor of Climate Change &
   Chief Scientist
International Arctic Research Center
University of Alaska Fairbanks
P.O. Box 757340 / 930 Koyukuk Drive
Fairbanks, Alaska 99775-7430
Phone: 907-474-2677
E-mail: jwalsh@iarc.uaf.edu

Richard Prentki
Oceanographer
Minerals Management Service
3801 Centerpoint Drive, Suite 500
Anchorage, Alaska 99503-5823
Phone: 907-334-5277
E-mail: Richard.Prentki@mms.gov

Imke Schramm
Water Environmental Research Center
University of Alaska Fairbanks
Fairbanks, Alaska 99775
Phone: 907-474-2783
E-mail: fnis@uaf.edu or
imkepots@rz.uni-potsdam.de

Caryn Smith
Oceanographer
Minerals Management Service
3801 Centerpoint Drive, Suite 500
Anchorage, Alaska 99503-5823
Phone: 907-334-5248
E-mail: caryn.smith@mms.gov

Nori Tanaka
Visiting Professor
International Arctic Research Center
University of Alaska Fairbanks
930 Koyukuk Dr./ P.O. Box 757340
Fairbanks, Alaska 99775-7340
Phone: 907-474-2687
E-mail: norit@iar.uaf.edu

Jia Wang
Research Associate Professor
International Arctic Research Center
University of Alaska Fairbanks
930 Koyukuk Dr., P.O. Box 757335
Fairbanks, Alaska 99775-7335
Phone: 907-474-2685
E-mail: jwang@iard.uaf.edu

Matthew Whitman
Fisheries Biologist – NPRA
Bureau of Land Management
1150 University Avenue
Fairbanks, Alaska 99709
Phone: 907-474-2249
E-mail: mwhitman@blm.gov

Daqing Yang
Water & Environment Research Center
University of Alaska Fairbanks
Fairbanks, Alaska 99775
Phone: 907-474-2468
E-mail: ffdy@uaf.edu

www.ingramcontent.com/pod-product-compliance
Lightning Source LLC
Chambersburg PA
CBHW080909290526
45795CB00007BA/2464